Timothy Findley's

THE WARS

Timothy Findley's

THE WARS

Dennis Garnhum

Timoth Findley's The Wars
first published 2008 by
Scirocco Drama
An imprint of J. Gordon Shillingford Publishing Inc.
© 2008 Dennis Garnhum
Based on the novel by Timothy Findley

Scirocco Drama Editor: Glenda MacFarlane
Cover design by Terry Gallagher/Doowah Design Inc.
Cover photo and author photo by David Cooper
Production photos by Trudie Lee
Printed and bound in Canada on 100% post-consumer recycled paper.

We acknowledge the financial support of the Manitoba Arts Council, The Canada
Council for the Arts and the Government of Canada through the Book Publishing
Industry Development Program (BPIDP) for our publishing program.

Production inquiries should be addressed to:
Playwrights Guild of Canada
215 Spadina Avenue, Suite 210
Toronto, ON M5T 2C7
416-703-0201

Library and Archives Canada Cataloguing in Publication

Garnhum, Dennis, 1967–
    Timothy Findley's The wars / Dennis Garnhum.

Stage adaptation of Timothy Findley's novel entitled The Wars.
ISBN 978-1-897289-33-4

    I. Findley, Timothy, 1930-2002. Wars. II. Title.

PS8613.A77T54 2008   C811'.6   C2008-903563-1

J. Gordon Shillingford Publishing
P.O. Box 86, RPO Corydon Avenue, Winnipeg, MB Canada R3M 3S3

For Bruce and Bill

Dennis Garnhum

Dennis Garnhum collaborated with Timothy Findley directing two of his world premieres at the Stratford Shakespeare Festival: *The Trials of Ezra Pound* and *Shadows*. Findley was one of Canada's most celebrated writers, earning international acclaim throughout his distinguished life. His renowned novel, *The Wars*, was published in 1977 and went on to win the Governor General's Award for Fiction. Findley had always wanted to see this novel adapted for the stage, and it was out of Garnhum's enormous admiration for him that the play was born.

Dennis Garnhum has served as the Artistic Director of Theatre Calgary since 2005. He has directed at theatres across North America including: the Shaw Festival, the Stratford Shakespeare Festival, Canadian Stage, the Manitoba Theatre Centre, and the Berkshire Theatre Festival. He has directed new work by Maureen Hunter, Steve LaPlante and Theresa Rebeck among others. *Timothy Findley's The Wars* debuted at Theatre Calgary in a co-production with the Playhouse Theatre Company of Vancouver in the fall of 2007.

Acknowledgements

The following people assisted in the development of *Timothy Findley's The Wars*, through workshops at Theatre Calgary's *Fuse: Petro-Canada's New Play Initiative* in 2006 and 2007, along with readings at the Playhouse Theatre Company, the Stratford Shakespeare Festival and in New York: Donald Adams, Shelley Ambrose, Paul Anthony, Christopher Austman, Brenden Averette, Brigit Beirne, Dave Bennett, Tamara Bernier, Beth Blickers, Diana Cafazzo, Joey Calveri, Don Carrier, Lara Jean Chorostecki, Paul Cowling, Tyrell Crews, Alexander Dodge, Rick Duthie, Jennie Esdale, Geoffrey Ewert, Louise Fagan, Randy Falcon, Martha Farrell, Tommy Foster, Shira Gilbert, Jeff Gladstone, Jonathan Goad, Adrienne Gould, Christian Goutsis, Jonathan Greenan, Elinor Holt, Christopher Hunt, Maureen Hunter, Kevin K. James, Rachael V. Johnston, Haysam Kadri, Scott Killian, Tim Koetting, Kevin Lamotte, Heather Laws, Trevor Leigh, Jennifer Lines, Christpher Loach, Heather Lea MacCallum, Jason MacDonald, William MacDonald, Anthony Malarky, Andrew Massingham, Joe Matheson, Tim Matheson, Hrothgar Mathews, Aly Mawji, Scott McAdam, Tom McBeath, Shawn McComb, Susan McNair Reid, Andrew McNee, Shelley McPherson, Brian Morey, Wendy Noel, Aaron Olney, Stafford Perry, Dawn Petten, Valerie Planche, Vanessa Porteous, Nathan Pronyshyn, Sandra Richmond, Kyle Rideout, Rick Rinder, Tyler Rive, Scott Roberts, Meg Roe, Eric Rose, Kerry Sandomirsky, Jordan Schartner, Joanna Schellenberg, Bruce Sellery, David Snelgrove, Matt Steinberg, Allan Stichbury, Haig Sutherland, Joseph Sutherland, Gillian Swan, Todd Talbot, Vern Thiessen, Nick van Burek, Kerry van der Griend, Mike Wasko, Shari Wattling, Frank Weldon, Erin Wells, Jeffrey Wetsch, William Whitehead, Brigit Wilson, and Kelly Wolf.

Special thanks to NEXEN for their generous support, to Glynis Leyshon, to Tom McCabe and to the Staff and Board of Directors of Theatre Calgary.

Production Information

Timothy Findley's The Wars was originally co-produced by Theatre Calgary and the Playhouse Theatre Company of Vancouver in the fall of 2007.

ROBERT ROSS .... Christian Goutsis
ROWENA, MARIAN .... Meg Roe
MR. ROSS .... Hrothgar Mathews
MRS. ROSS .... Kerry Sandomirsky
EVE .... Rachael V. Johnston
MACDONALD .... Kevin K. James
REGIS .... Stafford Perry
LEVITT .... Jeff Gladstone
PURCHAS .... Paul Anthony
TAFFLER .... Trevor Leigh
MARIA .... Erin Wells
ELLA .... Valerie Planche
LEATHER .... Paul Cowling
HARRIS .... Christopher Austman
COTÉ .... Andrew McNee
RODWELL .... Jordan Schartner

Directed by Dennis Garnhum
Set Design: Alan Stichbury
Costume Design: Kelly Wolf
Lighting Design: Kevin Lamotte
Original Music and Sound Design: Scott Killian
Projection Design: Tim Matheson
Production Dramaturg: Vanessa Porteous
Fight Director/Fight Captain: Kevin K. James
Stage Manager: Rick Rinder
Assistant Stage Manager: Ailsa Birnie
Apprentice Stage Manager: Heather Rycraft

Characters

ROBERT ROSS: a young man going off to war
ROWENA: his older sister
MR. ROSS: his father
MRS. ROSS: his mother
PRIVATE PURCHAS: lover of war
CAPTAIN TAFFLER: hero
SERGEANT MACDONALD: fearless
PRIVATE LEVITT: fearful
CAPTAIN LEATHER: overwhelmed leader
PRIVATE HARRIS: Nova Scotian who swims with whales
PRIVATE REGIS: boy too young for war
PRIVATE COTÉ: French Canadian collector of stained glass
SERGEANT RODWELL: dour animal devotee
STATION MASTER: at Lethbridge Station
EVE: maid to the Ross family
MARIA: madam who happens to be German
ELLA: prostitute of Lousetown
FLEMISH WOMAN: wandering in the fog
MARIAN: British nurse
JACKIE: Assistant to Marian
MAJOR MICKLE: leads charge against Robert
GUARD: stands watch over criminals

Time

World War One

A Note on Staging

The stage directions indicate elaborate notions for guiding purposes only. The play is intended to be performed simply and imaginatively. The roles may be double cast.

Act I

Scene One: Hesitation

> *1915. Empty train platform. Rain and darkness.*
>
> *ROBERT ROSS, 19, stands alone, suitcase by his side. Steam emits from an unseen departing train. STATION MASTER enters pushing a luggage trolly.*

MASTER: Young man? You just missed the eight-thirty. You tryin' to go north to Calgary?

ROBERT: Actually, I just came from there.

MASTER: Oh, I see.

ROBERT: I've been travelling. From Toronto.

MASTER: Toronto, eh? Well, you've made it to Lethbridge. Is that what you wanted?

ROBERT: Yes, sir.

MASTER: You a recruit? If you are, that's not a good sign, you know: losin' your company before you even make it to basic trainin'.

ROBERT: I didn't lose them. They walked on ahead. Which way to the base?

MASTER: Just follow that trail.

ROBERT: Thank you.

> *ROBERT remains still.*

MASTER: I suppose you've come here like all them others to join with the Field Artillery, huh?

ROBERT: That's right.

MASTER: I wish you luck, young man. The way they pour 'em in and outa here, it seems to me they're lookin' for a long, long war.

ROBERT: They promised it would be over by Christmas.

MASTER: Sure, young man.

STATION MASTER moves on, laughing.

They promised.

ROWENA: *(Off.)* You promised! Robert, you promised.

ROWENA fades into view sitting in a wicker wheelchair. She is an adult but behaves much younger. She is very small, with a lovely and pensive smile.

ROBERT: *(Remembering.)* Rowena.

ROWENA: When? You promised after lunch. When can I open my presents?

Rain slowly changes to sunshine.

MRS. ROSS: *(Off.)* Rowena, darling…where are you hiding?

MR. ROSS: *(Off.)* Robert? Where have you run ahead to?

ROBERT: We're over here, Father. Rowena has chosen a perfect spot.

MR. and MRS. ROSS and their maid, EVE, enter chatting and laughing. Mr. ROSS sets up a camera on a tripod.

MRS. ROSS: There you are.

ROWENA: Hello, Mother. Now may I open my presents?

MRS. ROSS: We want to take a picture first darling. We'll be quick about it. Just a few more minutes.

ROWENA: All right.

MRS. ROSS: How about here in the sunshine?

MR. ROSS: Wonderful.

MRS. ROSS: And let's not have the wheelchair, please. Robert?

> *MR. ROSS helps ROWENA to stand. ROBERT crosses over into the memory to assist. ROWENA cannot walk on her own very far. The wheelchair is placed out of the camera shot.*

MR ROSS: Will you do the honours, Eve?

EVE: I will try, sir.

> *MR. ROSS passes EVE the flashpot.*

MR. ROSS: Just hold this very steady. Up a little higher. Yes! Just like that.

EVE: I think I have it.

MR. ROSS: Hold very still—

MRS. ROSS: Smile everyone.

EVE: Here we go. 1 – 2 – 3 -

> *EVE takes the photograph.*

Beautiful!

MR ROSS: Thank you, Eve.

EVE: I hope I've done it properly.

MRS. ROSS: *(To ROWENA.)* Do you remember how old you are now, sweetheart?

ROWENA: Yes I do. I am twenty-five years old today.

MRS. ROSS: One quarter of a century. Very good. And they said she wouldn't make it past fifteen.

MR. ROSS: Our little miracle. Still with us.

ROWENA: Now is it time for presents?

MRS. ROSS: Yes, of course Rowena. You've been very patient.

                MRS. ROSS extends her gift.

ROWENA: I want to open Robert's first.

ROBERT: Are you expecting something from me?

ROWENA: Robert!!!

ROBERT: *(Laughing.)* Very well.

ROWENA: Hurray!!!

                He brings out a fabric covered gift.

ROBERT: I hope you like it. Close your eyes, young lady.

                ROWENA giggles. ROBERT pulls off the fabric to reveal two rabbits in a cage.

                Now you can open them.

ROWENA: Rabbits!

                Excited, she loses her balance. The men help her back into her wheelchair. ROBERT places the rabbits on her lap.

ROBERT: Here you go.

MRS. ROSS: Robert? You know she can't care for these on her own.

ROBERT: I know. I'll mind them for her, Mother.

MRS. ROSS: But you have too many animals already. You spend all your time with that horse of yours as it is…

ROWENA: Old Meggy!

MRS. ROSS: Yes, dear. Old Meggy. Well…they can't stay in the house.

ROBERT: We'll keep them in the barn loft. You don't have to worry.

ROWENA: *(To the rabbits.)* Ohhh…look at your pretty whiskers…

MRS. ROSS: I just wish you had asked before you went ahead. That's all.

ROBERT: Yes, Mother.

ROWENA: Thank you, Robert. This is the best present ever.

ROBERT: I thought you might like them.

ROWENA: I love them.

> *ROBERT and ROWENA look at each other. They share a quiet moment. MR. ROSS sees this and snaps a photograph.*

ROWENA: Father!

MR. ROSS: That one's for me.

EVE: Oh, Mr. Ross.

ROWENA: Do I get birthday cake today?

MRS. ROSS: Of course you do.

EVE: It's in the oven right now.

ROWENA: Can the rabbits have cake too, Eve?

> *Laughter.*

ROBERT: Whatever you like.

ROWENA: I want them to have their very own piece.

MRS. ROSS: *(Laughing.)* Well now, we'll have to see about that.

MR. ROSS: Oh, darling, look at the time. You're going to be late.

MRS. ROSS: Oh. I'm sorry, children. I have to leave for the station.

ROBERT: You're going?

MRS. ROSS: I'm afraid I must.

ROBERT: Do you have to? Even today?

MRS. ROSS: Someone has to, Robert. It's the least we can do for our young men. Wave them goodbye.

                Silence.

                Never mind. You two carry on.

ROBERT: Yes, Mother. We'll see you at dinner.

MR. ROSS: What about our gift?

MRS. ROSS: We'll save it for tonight. She wouldn't see it now, anyways. Not with the -

MR. ROSS: As you wish. *(To ROWENA.)* Happy birthday, Rowena.

MRS.ROSS: Happy birthday, darling.

EVE: Happy birthday, miss.

                MR. and MRS. ROSS exit, EVE following.

ROWENA: Robert?

ROBERT: Yes?

ROWENA: Can the rabbits stay forever?

ROBERT: Of course, Rowena.

ROWENA: Will you stay with me forever?

ROBERT: You're the only girl for me.

ROWENA: Besides Heather Lawson?

               She giggles.

ROBERT: Heather Lawson? That's over with. Guess what she
               did. Last week at a party she told me that a fellow
               named Joshua Sellery was in love with her and that
               meant she wanted me to fight him. Take him on the
               street and cause a ruckus. I asked her if she was in
               love with him or if she even liked him. Heather said
               she didn't. So I said, "then why should I fight him?"
               Heather didn't like that very much. "I never want
               to see you again," she said. All because I wouldn't
               fight a man she didn't love. So, she won't be coming
               around here any more.

ROWENA: I think that's for the best.

               *They laugh. ROBERT kneels beside ROWENA,
               confiding.*

ROBERT: So you see, now you really are the only girl for me.
               When I was just a baby, you were the first person I
               recall seeing. I was lying in my crib and as I woke
               I saw you glide your chair across the room to rest
               beside me. We stared and stared at each other.

ROWENA: I don't remember.

ROBERT: I do. I remember thinking that you were my
               mother.

               He laughs.

ROWENA: I remember the day I met your horse.

ROBERT: Old Meggy's your favourite, isn't she?

ROWENA: Oh yes she is!

ROBERT: Why do you love her so much?

ROWENA: Because you do.

ROBERT: And now she'll have friends to talk to. Should we
             take the rabbits to the barn and introduce them?

ROWENA: Yes, please! *(Shouting out.)* Hey Meggy! We've got a
             surprise for you! Close your eyes.

             They start to go. ROWENA stops.

             Robert?

ROBERT: Yes?

ROWENA: Promise me the rabbits can stay forever.

ROBERT: Of course, Rowena.

ROWENA: Promise me you will stay forever.

             Thunder. Sunshine turns back to rain.

MASTER: *(Offstage.)* Young man?

             Silence. ROWENA fades away.

ROBERT: I promise.

             *The STATION MASTER returns. He shines a
             flashlight at ROBERT.*

MASTER: Young man! You can't stay here all night. Get goin'
             now.

             ROBERT picks up the suitcase. He decides to walk.

ROBERT: *(To himself.)* Onward, soldier.

Scene Two: Basic Training

> *Training camp—outdoors. Men in civilian clothes rush on as if in combat. This breaks down into horseplay and laughter.*

TAFFLER: Break it up. Break it up.

> *They do.*

MACDONALD: *(Calling out.)* Mail call.

> *Distributing the mail as he calls out.*

> Regis—

REGIS: Right here. *(Taking letter.)*

MACDONALD: Levitt—

LEVITT: My books. *(Taking package.)* Thanks, MacDonald.

MACDONALD: Purchas—

PURCHAS: Hellllooo, Cindy! *(Taking package.)*

MACDONALD: Ross—

ROBERT: Here. *(Taking package.)* Thank you.

MACDONALD: Conliffe…Conliffe?

> *MACDONALD continues to distribute mail.*

PURCHAS: Robert Ross? Is that you?

ROBERT: Yes.

PURCHAS: What in the hell are you doing here? How long you been hiding?

ROBERT: Well, I've been here for awhile now.

PURCHAS: I didn't know you signed up. Robert Ross in basic training. What in the hell?

They shake hands.

ROBERT: Clifford, isn't it?

PURCHAS: That's right, Clifford Purchas. Well of all things! It's one hell of a surprise to see you. I gotta say you don't seem like the fighting type.

ROBERT: I didn't realize they would be sending us to Alberta for training.

PURCHAS: Remember back in cadets? It sure is a lot different than those days. Real guns and real bullets. No playing around here. They explained that to you, I hope.

ROBERT: Yes, thanks. I know that much. But do they have to yell at us all the time? I've never been fond of noise. I hated that about cadets.

PURCHAS: Is that why you would blush on parade all the time?

ROBERT: What do you mean?

PURCHAS: A few of the fellas noticed it. We used to call you "Red."

ROBERT: I don't know that I like that.

PURCHAS: It's a compliment, Ross. It's hard to dislike a man who blushes.

> *Holds out his newly opened package.*

Cookie?

> *ROBERT accepts.*

What did you get in your parcel? Anything good?

ROBERT: It's from my mother. There's a whole lot in here. Chocolate...socks...she's probably even packed me a—

Pulls out a scarf.

Scarf! Would you look at that!

PURCHAS: A scarf? In the summer?

ROBERT: My mother thinks everything north of Toronto is cold. And if it's west, it must be freezing. She thinks I've stepped outside the bounds of civilization where people don't wear clothes or eat cooked meat.

PURCHAS: But a scarf? In August?

ROBERT: She thinks it snows year round out here.

PURCHAS: That's impossible.

TAFFLER passes by with a crate of bottles, exits.

Well, I sure like this place. Have you ever seen such a sky? And the, what do you call those, the—sort of valleys?

ROBERT: The coulees?

PURCHAS: Right. What a sight. Never seen hills like that. They're like mountains that go down rather than up.

ROBERT: I like to go running in the coulees.

PURCHAS: You do?

ROBERT: And last night I ended up running with a coyote.

PURCHAS: A coyote, eh?

ROBERT: Yes. It just appeared ahead of me while I was running so I decided to follow. I stayed back, of course, so it wouldn't see me. Eventually the coyote started drinking at a pool of water. When it moved on, it threw its head back and howled. Then it turned and looked directly at me. It was telling me that it was my turn to drink. That coyote had known I was there the whole time! It barked three times, and then trotted off towards the sun.

PURCHAS starts howling like a coyote.

CAPTAIN TAFFLER, tall and built for playing sports, begins throwing stones at bottles lined up on a board just out of sight. His shirt is hanging at his waist.

All right, all right. Be quiet.

PURCHAS: What?

ROBERT: Look.

TAFFLER throws another stone. The bottle smashes perfectly.

Who is that?

PURCHAS: Don't you know? That's Captain Eugene Taffler you idiot. He's already been to France. He was wounded over there. Before the war, he was a Varsity all-round athlete.

ROBERT: Oh.

PURCHAS: Everyone talks about him. He's a real hero. Let's go over.

ROBERT: Maybe we should leave him to—

They go over. TAFFLER hits another bottle.

TAFFLER: Are you wondering what in hell I'm doing? Welllll…

He throws another stone to demonstrate.

That's what I'm doing. Killing bottles.

ROBERT: Oh.

TAFFLER: I have to keep my arm in.

PURCHAS: Yes, sir! I've heard about you in those Varsity games.

ROBERT: What a pity!

TAFFLER: A pity, Mister...?

ROBERT: Ross, sir.

TAFFLER: And why a pity, Mister Ross?

ROBERT: Oh, I don't know, sir.

PURCHAS: Maybe that we aren't all playing ball.

TAFFLER: Yes, I guess that is a pity.

TAFFLER fires again.

You can't be too prepared, take it from me. The distance between our lines and theirs is often no more than a hundred yards. Did you know that?

PURCHAS: No, sir.

TAFFLER: One hundred yards. All you get in this war is one man against another. Like this:

He fires again. LEVITT and MACDONALD approach.

MACDONALD: Captain Taffler, are you going back tonight?

LEVITT: MacDonald and I are up for another round.

TAFFLER: Sure thing, Levitt. I've demolished enough bottles for today.

To ROBERT and PURCHAS.

You fellas ever been to Lousetown?

PURCHAS: Lousetown? I haven't heard of it.

MACDONALD: Well, you aren't going to find it on any map. A few houses dangling on the edge of a coulee.

PURCHAS: What goes on there?

LEVITT: Anything you like, thanks to Maria and her girls.

PURCHAS: Ohhh, I see.

LEVITT: It's all I think about.

TAFFLER: Why don't you come with us?

MACDONALD: You'll end up there sooner or later.

PURCHAS: I'm in.

ROBERT: Clifford, I'm not sure—

PURCHAS: You're not afraid are you?

ROBERT: Well…

LEVITT: Come on—it's simple: either you 'do' or you 'don't'.

PURCHAS: Remember, Robert: Real guns, real bullets.

MACDONALD: Which is it: 'do' or 'don't'?

ROBERT: I…I do.

TAFFLER: That's the spirit. Think of it as part of your basic training, Ross.

PURCHAS: Fellas, lead on!

The men howl like coyotes. Arms go over shoulders. They are frozen in time for a second or two.

When they come alive again they are drunk.

(l to r): Paul Anthony (Purchas), Chistian Goutsis (Ross), Trevor Leigh (Taffler), Kevin K. James (Macdonald) and Jeff Gladstone (Levitt).

Scene Three: Jumping the Gun

> *MARIA's in Lousetown. MACDONALD hands ROBERT a bottle.*

MACDONALD: Finish it.

> *ROBERT does—draining it dry. ROBERT hands PURCHAS the bottle to hold up and then mimes tossing a stone at it.*

TAFFLER: Welcome boys to Lousetown's famous Dry Goods store. Don't let the name scare you. It may be 'dry goods' up front, but I promise you that once you get in the back there's plenty of 'wet goods'. But choose carefully. If you pick the 'spoiled goods' you'll end up out here with the rest of the garbage.

PURCHAS: If they're all naked in the parlour, I'll faint!

> *MARIA, a German madam with bright copper hair, appears.*

TAFFLER: Ah, Maria.

> *MARIA gathers up PURCHAS and ROBERT.*

MARIA: Well, good effning, chentlemen. Follow me. Right this way.

> *MARIA and the men move into a parlor filled with women and a few cowboys. Lilac wallpaper covers the walls. MACDONALD pours drinks. LEVITT picks up a girl and carries her to a chair, sits her down and kneels between her legs.*

LEVITT: I can see it! Lordy, Lordy! I can see it! Look at that!

> *A girl turns on the phonograph. The music consists of a thumping piano and a wailing cornet. Everyone dances. TAFFLER notices that ROBERT is alone so he walks a woman, ELLA, over to him.*

TAFFLER: Ross, do me a favour?

ROSS: Yes, sir.

TAFFLER: *(Laughs to himself.)* "Yes, sir."…Will you keep this young girl company? See that she is properly taken care of.

ROSS: *(Shaken.)* Oh…yes, sir. I will.

TAFFLER: Good work, soldier.

               TAFFLER walks away, leaving them alone.

ELLA: Hi there, I'm Ella. *(Silence.)* You got a name?

ROBERT: Yes. I'm Robert.

ELLA: You wanna trot?

ROBERT: Trot?

ELLA: Dance.

ROBERT: I don't think I know how.

ELLA: I'll show ya.

               ELLA places her arms around his neck and presses her pelvis hard against his groin.

               Well, ya gotta move!

               They dance awkwardly. ELLA pulls ROBERT in close while dancing. TAFFLER dances past and gestures encouragement to ROBERT that he is doing well.

               Music ends. Everyone applauds.

MARIA: Chentlemen. It's time. Off you go.

               The women escort their men off. ROBERT hesitates. ELLA waits.

ELLA: Hey kid. My room's upstairs. Ya wanna go?

               He does not move.

The sooner we start, the more time we'll have, if you get me.

ELLA moves to ROBERT.

Ya wanna fool around in here first? We can take it nice and slow. You call the shots. Anythin' special you'd like? I mean—here we are and everythin'.

She takes off his boots.

See, that didn't hurt ya.

Pulls off his shirt.

My, my. You hidin' your nice little body from me? Look, this is what I'm paid for. To make ya happy.

You want to touch me, don't ya? Why don't ya try? Just feel anywhere.

She offers her body. He does not move.

In my whole life I never met a man who had so little to say.

She laughs as she runs her finger over his lips.

Your little tongue in there? You're a nice lookin' kid an' we shouldn't just be sittin' here. Why don't you let me…

She puts her hand down his pants.

Oh. I see.

She removes her hand and crosses to the wash basin. She rinses her hand.

Take them off an' I'll clean you up.

Still no response.

Well—at least we know you're alive. You oughtn't be ashamed, you know. There's lotsa fellows do what you done: jump the gun.

She grins. ROBERT looks up, smiles.

ROBERT: Jump the gun?

ELLA: Yeh. Ka-pow! Usually happens the first time. An' I can't even begin to tell ya how many fellas can't do nothin'. Look, we got all night. Give yourself a little rest an' then…how's bout that?

           Silence.

           Dontcha un'erstand? —If you don't do me I don't get paid!

ROBERT: How would anyone know?

ELLA: She'll know from the way you walk. Guys that done it got a way o' walkin'. And guys that haven't got a way of walkin' to. She c'n tell.

ROBERT: But what difference does it make? I can fake the walk on my way out. You just show me how.

ELLA: We ain't workin' if we don't do it, she says. Don't ask me. It's her rule. Everybody's s'posed to enjoy themselves. "Minkle! Minkle! Eve'body gotta minkle 'n' screw!" She says if you go away unlaid, her house'll get a bad reputation. That's her rule.

           Sounds come from the other room. ELLA stands up and crosses to the wall. She moves a lilac in the lilac wallpaper revealing a peephole.

ROBERT: What are you doing?

ELLA: Shhh! Hush and come here. *(Giggles.)* Look! This might give ya a few ideas. Show ya how it's done…

           ROBERT looks through the hole. We see what he sees: the men having their way with the women. The sex is physical and animated. Firelight and shadows. ROBERT turns away. ELLA holds his head to the hole.

Watch, kid. I'm serious.

ROBERT sees TAFFLER in the group. TAFFLER moans in ecstasy.

ROBERT: No…

ROBERT pulls back.

ELLA: Kid, calm down.

ELLA touches him. He moves away.

ROBERT: Not like this.

MARIA and another prostitute enter the room.

Not like this.

ELLA: I didn't mean to push ya too far—if ya ain't up for it—then ya ain't up for it.

ROBERT: *(Sudden burst of anger.)* "I ain't".

ELLA: Fine. Get outta here…and don't you come back ever. Ya hear?

ROBERT gathers his clothes and stumbles out. ELLA throws his boots after him.

PROSTITUTE: Yeah…get lost ya coward!

The room goes silent.

ELLA: I know, I know. I don't get paid.

Scene Four: Marching Orders

Barracks. Clean uniforms hang on pegs about the room. Bugle call. The men enter in their underclothes.

LEVITT: My bones can't take all this beating. Basic training is killing me.

PURCHAS: I'm not used to getting up this early.

LEVITT: Several times I've complained, but no one listens.

MACDONALD: Or cares, Levitt. Quit your whining and get dressed.

> *TAFFLER enters in full uniform.*

Company! Attention.

> *The men stand and salute.*

TAFFLER: Good morning men, as you were.

> *The men begin to dress.*

I have good news. Your training will be completed this week.

MACDONALD: I thought we had until the end of the month to go, sir.

TAFFLER: You're ready now so we're shipping you out early.

PURCHAS: No kidding, sir?

TAFFLER: That's right. We head east in five days. By month's end we'll be in Belgium.

PURCHAS: Well, Levitt. That's worth getting up for.

TAFFLER: Before you know it, you'll be putting all of this training into action.

> *The men cheer. TAFFLER notices ROBERT who is avoiding eye contact.*

Hello, Ross.

ROBERT: Hello, Captain.

> *ROBERT salutes.*

TAFFLER: As you were. So, Ross?

ROBERT: Yes, sir?

TAFFLER: So?

ROBERT: What, sir?

TAFFLER: Tell me about the other night.

ROBERT: Oh, the other night.

TAFFLER: Wet, dry or spoiled? What was the final verdict?

ROBERT: It turned out…just exactly as I would have predicted.

TAFFLER: Good, good.

Silence. TAFFLER starts to walk away.

ROBERT: Sir—can I ask you something?

TAFFLER: Shoot.

ROBERT: When I get over there…

TAFFLER: Yes?

ROBERT: How do I ensure…

TAFFLER: What?

ROBERT: Victory. A big word, I know.

TAFFLER: Say more.

ROBERT: Well…they're making me a Second Lieutenant.

TAFFLER: Yes, I know. Good for you, Ross.

ROBERT: Not really, sir.

TAFFLER: What do you mean?

ROBERT: You and I both know how this happened. My family name guaranteed it. I didn't earn the title, I was more or less promised it.

TAFFLER: Be that as it may. I didn't exactly deserve the title 'hero'.

ROBERT: But you are, sir—

TAFFLER: Ross, I was a good soldier over there. I don't deny that. But do you know why they call me a hero? Because I was wounded and survived.

ROSS: But that makes you a—

TAFFLER: A hero. Sure, Ross. I'm a hero. But I'm going back to prove it. For myself. Just like you'll prove that you deserve to be a Second Lieutenant. You're a bit scared then?

ROSS: Yes, sir. Terrified.

TAFFLER: Good. Some of these men are fearless. They'll be dead in the first weeks of battle.

ROBERT: But will anyone actually follow my instructions?

TAFFLER: People won't pat you on the back, but they will do what you command.

ROBERT: I'm not so sure that Canada should be relying on me to lead the way.

TAFFLER: Of course it should. It's clear to me. You'll succeed.

ROBERT: Thank you, sir.

            Confidentially.

TAFFLER: I should tell you that we're shipping out early because of necessity—if you follow.

ROBERT: Sir?

TAFFLER: They need us over there right away.

ROBERT: I see.

TAFFLER: Don't tell the others. It's sooner than I would have liked.

ROBERT: Oh.

TAFFLER: You and your men will need to be at the ready.

ROBERT: Yes, sir. Not killing…just throwing stones…

TAFFLER: Pardon?

ROBERT: Nothing.

TAFFLER: Oh—and one other thing. Here's the best piece of advice I have. Only jump the gun once.

ROBERT: *(Feigns ignorance.)* Jump the gun?

TAFFLER: Ka-pow. Believe me, Ross…I jumped the gun the first time too. And then I figured it out.

                ROBERT smiles. TAFFLER adjusts ROBERT's tie.

                Better. Much better.

                The room has become a sea of bright new uniforms. The men look sharp and awfully proud.

                Gentlemen—

                Men look to TAFFLER.

                Welcome to the war.

                Men cheer as they toss their hats into the air.

Scene Five: Send Off

                Dockside. Cold night. Patriotic music is heard as the soldiers carry their packs, preparing to depart. Parents and wives say their goodbyes.

                MR. and MRS. ROSS enter. MRS. ROSS sees ROBERT and stops moving. She has been drinking.

MRS. ROSS: There he is. I can't.

MR. ROSS: What do you mean?

MRS. ROSS: I can't.

MR. ROSS: You wanted to come.

MRS. ROSS: Of course I wanted to come. It's just that—

MR. ROSS: We've travelled all this way. Now let's go over and say our goodbyes. We don't have much time.

MRS. ROSS: You go ahead. I'll wait back here.

MR. ROSS: Come say goodbye. You're being ridiculous.

MRS. ROSS: Don't!

MR. ROSS: How will I explain where you are?

MRS. ROSS: Don't force me. Please—don't force me…

She hides in the crowd. After a moment, MR. ROSS goes to ROBERT.

ROBERT: Father, you made it!

MR. ROSS: Robert! And with little time to spare, it seems. Looks like they're nearly done loading the ship.

ROBERT: We have a few minutes.

MR. ROSS: Good to see you, son.

ROBERT: And you too, Father.

MR. ROSS: How was the train from Alberta?

ROBERT: Endless. Five days or so. I lost count.

Awkward silence.

What do you think?

MR. ROSS: Think?

ROBERT: How do I look?

MR. ROSS: You look like a soldier. And like a grown man.

> *Silence.*

Strange.

> *Silence.*

I always thought you'd be joining me in the company. But I guess commerce can't compete with war. I still have hope that you'll join me after it's all over.

ROBERT: Yes, Father.

MR. ROSS: My son a Second Lieutenant.

ROBERT: Amazing what a last name will do for you.

MR. ROSS: Yes, well, nonetheless. Surname or not, seeing you do something I've never done—it's... well... strange...and mighty impressive.

> *MR. ROSS presents a small wood box to ROBERT.*

There it is. The best that money can buy.

> *ROBERT opens box. Discovers a gun.*

ROBERT: Would you look at that!

MR. ROSS: Did I buy the right one?

ROBERT: A Webley Mark Six. Yes, that's what they told us to get.

MR. ROSS: It doesn't seem right to me that officers have to supply their own pistols. Oh. I forgot to buy bullets.

ROBERT: That's okay, they supply those. And thanks again for the uniform.

MR. ROSS: You're welcome. That must be why they call it the 'People's Army.' There's something else in the box.

ROBERT takes out a photograph.

You and Rowena. I thought you'd like it with you.

ROBERT: Oh.

Sound of a horn from the ship.

I have to go.

MR. ROSS: Yes…well…Robert, I'm sorry your Mother couldn't make the journey. She intended to but—

ROBERT: I understand.

Silence.

I promise to write every week.

MR. ROSS: Please do. Good luck, son.

An uncomfortable handshake.

ROBERT walks away quickly. MR. ROSS finds MRS. ROSS. ROBERT notices his parents together. He watches, unnoticed. MRS. ROSS reveals a flask.

MRS. ROSS: Just like Rowena.

MR. ROSS: No, not like Rowena.

MRS. ROSS: You wait and see. We'll lose him. Just like Rowena.

MR.ROSS: Don't say it. Don't think it.

MRS. ROSS: You'll see.

They go as PURCHAS enters.

PURCHAS: Robert? There you are!

A large crate is brought in containing a horse.

White light from inside the crate represents the animal.

Would you look at that? Last chance to change your mind.

ROBERT: Not me. I don't plan on giving up this soon.

Clifford—just one thing. Stick close by. I'm prepared for the fighting but crossing the Atlantic I'm not so sure about.

PURCHAS and ROBERT exit as the horse crate is lifted into the air and loaded onto the ship. Men guide the box with ropes that hang down from the crate. This loading is a group effort and not particularily well managed. We hear the horse within.

Scene Six: Sea Horses and Whales

Deck of the ship. The seas are rough.

PRIVATE HARRIS, a young man from the east coast with a pronounced accent, is leaning on the railing. He stares at the sea as other soldiers move past in the frigid air. He has a slight cough.

Further along the deck, ROBERT enters covering his mouth. CAPTAIN LEATHER follows directly behind him also on the brink of sickness.

LEATHER: You see, Lieutenant? You see? I took you down there in the hold to see for yourself.

ROBERT: Yes, Captain Leather. It's filthy. The condition of the horses down there is horrific. The manure... unbelievable.

LEATHER: Absolutely. And now the officer in charge has fallen ill. Until he's recovered, I'm assigning his duties to you. Keep watch over that mess down there. See that it doesn't get worse.

ROBERT: Yes, sir. Well, then the first thing we should do is to get a clean-up crew—

LEATHER: What?

ROBERT: The manure, sir. The flies are breeding in it. And in the meantime, I'll have the hatches opened, to kill off the flies with the cold.

LEATHER: What in hell are you talking about? Men are getting sick by the dozens. We can't drop the temperature anywhere. We shouldn't even be out here in this cold.

ROBERT: But, sir…the horses…and the flies…

LEATHER: Horses! These damn beasts shouldn't even be on this ship! And when we get to England, I mean to have my say about that. Transporting men and animals in the same vessel! It's barbarous! I've assigned Gunner Purchas to assist you—but that's all. The fewer men involved with those damned horses, the better. I don't want my soldiers coming down with any barnyard diseases! Just keep the beggars alive until we dock!

> *LEATHER exits. ROBERT stands helpless.*
> *MACDONALD and LEVITT enter and approach*
> *HARRIS. ROBERT observes.*

MACDONALD: Hey, Gunner. Whatcha doing out here in the cold? Looking for something?

HARRIS: I am actually.

MACDONALD: What could possibly be out there?

HARRIS: A whale.

MACDONALD: Don't tell me you've actually seen one?

HARRIS: No, not yet.

MACDONALD: 'Not yet.' Not likely ever. They're all down south, anyway, you know.

HARRIS: You never can tell.

MACDONALD: 'You never can tell'. It takes all kinds. Call me when Moby Dick appears.

> As LEVITT and MACDONALD exit, they laugh together.

LEVITT: Moby Dick?

MACDONALD: I know…I just thought of it…

> HARRIS coughs.

ROBERT: Hello, soldier. Cold night.

HARRIS: Hello, sir. I don't mind it.

ROBERT: Any sightings so far?

HARRIS: What do you mean, sir?

ROBERT: I heard tell that if you keep your eyes glued to the sea you might glimpse a whale or two.

HARRIS: You've heard that?

ROBERT: Of course. Haven't you?

HARRIS: Yes, sir, I have. Back home I'd sit by the shore and wait. If I held on and waited long enough—sometimes into the wee hours of the night, I would get the greatest show on earth.

ROBERT: Where's home, Gunner?

HARRIS: Cape Breton, Nova Scotia. No place finer. I haven't been anywhere else much, but I'm sure of it.

ROBERT: I haven't spent much time on the water.

HARRIS: How are you finding it?

ROBERT: Well…I've stopped slamming into the sides of the boat every time a big wave crashes up. And I've

	just heard about something called sea legs. I think I'm finally starting to get a pair of those.
HARRIS:	Good, because a gigantic storm is coming.
ROBERT:	It is? And how do you figure that?
HARRIS:	Those waves. They tell me all I need to know.
	HARRIS coughs.
ROBERT:	You don't sound all that well.
HARRIS:	No, not so good.
ROBERT:	What's your name, Gunner?
HARRIS:	Harris, sir.
ROBERT:	Nice to meet you, Harris. I'm Robert—I mean Lieutenant Ross. Now Harris, a gift to you from my mother.
	Taking off his scarf.
HARRIS:	But sir—
ROBERT:	I hate scarves so you might as well get some use from it.
HARRIS:	Thank you, sir. That's very kind. You sure?
ROBERT:	Yes. It will please my mother.
HARRIS:	All right then.
	HARRIS puts on the scarf. He has a coughing fit.
	With my lungs—and my luck—this could turn into just about anything.
ROBERT:	Maybe it's best if you head on in.
HARRIS:	I'm a Maritimer. We survive most things. What about you?

ROBERT: People from Toronto prefer the land.

HARRIS: Maybe *you* should go in, sir.

               They laugh.

ROBERT: I do like it out here. Peaceful in an odd way. And I wouldn't mind seeing a whale or two. Anything to distract myself from the horses below. Am I in your way?

HARRIS: Two sets of eyes are better than one.

ROBERT: Okay, then. Together we'll keep watch for a school of whales to come along.

HARRIS: Pod. We're looking for a pod of whales.

ROBERT: Oh, I see. A pod of whales.

HARRIS: Yes, sir.

               Silence. They watch.

ROBERT: Do you miss your family back in Cape Breton?

HARRIS: No, sir. Not really. I'm an only child. My mother died when I was three and I don't see my father all that much. He makes fishing boats. I was sort of adopted by the sea. What about you?

ROBERT: Well…

               PURCHAS approaches with a lit lantern.

PURCHAS: Hey, Robert. I mean—sir! I'm sorry to have to tell you, but one of the horses has broken its leg.

ROBERT: Oh.

PURCHAS: That means it has to be shot.

ROBERT: Well, then do it.

PURCHAS: What?

ROBERT: *(Attempting authority.)* Do it, Clifford. That's an order.

PURCHAS: I'm sorry, Robert—Lieutenant—can't.

ROBERT: And why not?

PURCHAS: Only officers carry sidearms, sir. And you're the officer in charge, sir. So you'll have to do it.

ROBERT: Yes. Right.

            ROBERT looks to the sea—terrified.

HARRIS: Sir? Are you okay, sir?

ROBERT: Yes. Just a chill.

HARRIS: Would you like us to come with you?

ROBERT: Yes.

PURCHAS: I'll lead the way.

            As the men descend into the hold, ROBERT checks for his gun at his waist. The noise of frightened horses is overpowering.

            The lantern picks up the crouching figure of a distraught teenager, PRIVATE REGIS. He has been weeping and his face is streaked with dust.

ROBERT: Regis? What are you doing down here?

REGIS: We shall all be drowned, sir.

ROBERT: Who in their right mind let you into the army? You can't be old enough.

REGIS: I lied to get in, sir. I lied.

ROBERT: What?

REGIS: Who cares now? We're all going to drown, sir.

ROBERT: No, Regis, no.

Bright white light shoots up from below representing the fallen horse.

PURCHAS: Here's the horse.

ROBERT takes his gun and tries to aim. He is uncertain as to which part to fire at.

Careful, sir!

ROBERT steps aside. He takes aim. His arm wavers. He hesitates.

Just do it, sir. You have to do it.

ROBERT: I can hear you. Please—just give me a minute.

MRS. ROSS enters into this world.

MRS. ROSS: It's time, Robert.

ROBERT: Mother?

MRS. ROSS: You know you have to do it.

ROBERT: Do what, Mother?

MRS. ROSS: Kill the rabbits.

ROBERT: What?! The rabbits? Why?

MRS. ROSS: Because they were hers.

ROBERT: But that can't possibly make sense.

MRS. ROSS: It's your responsibility.

ROBERT: I know. I'll look after them.

MRS. ROSS: Don't be ridiculous, Robert. Gracious. You're a grown man. And you assured me that you'd watch over Rowena.

ROBERT: Mother—

MR. ROSS appears with the cage of rabbits.

Can't we give them away? Father? They haven't done anything wrong.

MRS. ROSS: They'll only remind us of her.

MR. ROSS: Just do what Mother says.

He offers the cage to ROBERT.

MRS. ROSS: Take them, Robert. Take them away and destroy them.

ROBERT: They belonged to Rowena. I won't do it.

MRS. ROSS: Robert—

PURCHAS: Robert?

ROBERT: I'll keep them with me.

ROBERT takes the cage from MR. ROSS.

MR. ROSS: It's for the best.

ROBERT: You won't have to see them. I'll care for them—

MRS. ROSS: She died trying to reach those damned rabbits. If you won't kill them, we'll take them back. Oh, you stubborn...

MR. ROSS tries to take the cage back. He does not expect what follows: ROBERT struggles with him over the cage. At the same time, a sudden ship movement causes the horses to scream and PURCHAS, REGIS and HARRIS to fall.

MR. ROSS: Come on now.

MRS. ROSS: Please.

MR. ROSS: Stop this, Robert. Let go.

PURCHAS: Watch out.

ROBERT falls to the ground, hurting his shoulder.

MR. ROSS has the cage.

MR. ROSS: It won't bring her back.

PURCHAS: Get up, Robert. Get it done.

MR. and MRS. ROSS disappear.

HARRIS: Just be very quick about it, sir. Just be very cool and quick.

PURCHAS moves closer with the lamp. REGIS is sobbing. ROBERT fires at the horse.

PURCHAS: You didn't kill it!

ROBERT fires again and sinks to his knees. He speaks to the horse.

ROBERT: Damn it, shut up, damn it—SHUT UP!!!

ROBERT shoots over and over until his gun is empty. The horse becomes silent. White light fades away.

HARRIS pulls the gun from ROBERT's hands. Robert continues the clicking gesture without the gun.

After a moment.

HARRIS: Shall we go back up, sir?

ROBERT: No. Not yet, anyway.

An embarrassed silence.

If this damn ship would sell us one, I'd buy us all a drink.

REGIS: No thank you, sir. I promised my mother I wouldn't.

Scene Seven: Fog and Mud

Flanders. Distance explosions and gun fire.

Fog rolls in. A Flemish woman appears—searching and calling out for something indecipherable. She moves off. ROBERT emerges through the fog with MACDONALD and PURCHAS. They are slogging through mud.

MACDONALD: Have you ever seen such thick fog?

PURCHAS: You could slice it with a knife.

ROBERT: I just hope the men behind us can keep up.

MACDONALD: I bet mud is a Flemish word. We should call this country "Mudland."

The peasant approaches. She speaks to them in Flemish, waving her arms excitedly.

FLEMISH: Militairen. Hebt u mijn koeien genomen? Wat u met mijn koeien hebt gedaan? U hebt hen genomen en ik weet niet waar zij zijn. Mijn koeien! Waar zijn mijn koeien?

"Soldiers. Have you taken my cows? What have you done with my cows? You have taken them and I do not know where they are. My cows! Where are my cows?"

ROBERT: Where did she come from?

PURCHAS: And what is she saying?

ROBERT: It's gibberish to me.

MACDONALD: Maybe she escaped from the asylum.

Laughter from the men.

FLEMISH: *(Switching to french.)* Vous me comprenez mieux en Français. Avez-vous pris mes vaches? Qu'avez-vous fait avec mes vaches?

"Maybe you understand me better in French. Have you taken my cows? What have you done with my cows?"

ROBERT: Vaches? Something about cows. What about cows?

MACDONALD: Can't you speak English?

FLEMISH: Enklesh! Enklesh! Vous etes anglais? Maudit anglais!

The woman screams and throws her hat down.

Maudit anglais! Ce sont tous des assassins!

MACDONALD: Calm down, old woman! Calm down!

ROBERT: Madame! Je suis Canadian! Je ne parle pas francais!

FLEMISH: Maudit anglais!

The woman picks up her hat and wanders off, disgusted.

ROBERT: Well—we tried.

PURCHAS: She navigates this fog like it's a clear day.

MACDONALD: Too bad though, that she can't keep track of her own cows! It's not our fault.

They walk on through the mud.

ROBERT: Keep your eyes open wide for any barns or houses along this road where we can stop for the night. We've traveled enough for today in this impossible weather.

MACDONALD: I could run ahead and scout out options, sir.

ROBERT: No. No one's going ahead. I'm beginning to wonder if anyone's coming behind. Maybe we should stop and let the others catch up.

They stop. The sound of wings, of splashing, of moving water.

PURCHAS: What if we've gone and taken the wrong turn?

ROBERT: Wrong turn? No, just wait. The others will catch up. What are those noises?

PURCHAS: Birds.

ROBERT: I'd be surprised if any birds had survived in this place.

Sound of something flying up from the ditch.

What can be keeping the others?

More sound of wings and squawks.

Name all the birds you can think of.

PURCHAS: Sir?

MACDONALD: Storks.

ROBERT: I'm being serious.

MACDONALD: So am I, sir. I'm sorry, but I just can't think of any besides storks. I'm too damn cold…

PURCHAS: What about ducks?

ROBERT: Ducks? Maybe they're flying south and need a place to rest. That's what it is. They're resting in this field.

LEVITT: *(A distant shout.)* Ha…loooo…

ROBERT: Good, they're here. Ha…looooooo!

LEVITT: *(Shouting.)* Don't move.

ROBERT: *(Calling back.)* Okay.

MACDONALD: What can be wrong?

ROBERT: We'll soon find out. *(Calling.)* Who is it?

LEVITT: *(Calling.)* Me!

MACDONALD: Who the hell is 'me'?

> *LEVITT emerges from the fog. He is soaking wet and covered in mud. His hat is missing.*

LEVITT: Me! Levitt.

ROBERT: Levitt? You were supposed to be at the rear. You shouldn't have left your post.

MACDONALD: Who's protecting the two wagons back there carrying rum?

LEVITT: I'm sorry sir, but I had to come forward. A man and his horse—

ROBERT: What happened?

LEVITT: —went through the dike, sir.

ROBERT: What dike?

LEVITT: *This* dike.

> *The men exchange looks.*

PURCHAS: What are you talking about?

LEVITT: Somewhere back there you took the wrong turn, sir, and you've taken us out onto this dike and it's slowly collapsing.

ROBERT: Collapsing?

LEVITT: There's a break probably a hundred to a hundred and fifty yards behind us filling with water. When the rider came through it was six feet across. When I came through it was ten feet across. By now it might be fifteen or twenty.

MACDONALD: So what now, Lieutenant?

ROBERT: Let's head back.

PURCHAS: Good idea.

Sound of wings, splashing.

ROBERT: What *is* all that?

LEVITT: You mean the birds, sir?

ROBERT: Yes.

LEVITT: It's the crows.

ROBERT: Crows? What on earth are so many crows doing out here?

LEVITT just looks at him.

PURCHAS: Levitt?

LEVITT: They're eating.

ROBERT: Eating?

PURCHAS: Eating what?

LEVITT: Well, everywhere…in the water, in the mud… there are… *(A helpless gesture.)*…all the dead.

Silence.

MACDONALD: Let's get out of here.

The men begin to exit, retracing their steps.

ROBERT retrieves his sack. When he turns back, the men have disappeared in the fog.

ROBERT, alone, becomes disoriented.

He hears something: The sound of water. Wanting to avoid it, he walks away in the other direction.

Suddenly:

His feet sink into the mud —

First to the knees, then to his waist.

He falls back onto his shoulders.

He holds on with his elbows.

He continues to sink in the mud up to his neck.

He can't speak. The only sound is that of his intense breathing. And of crows.

Eventually:

He leans forward. He begins to rock, front-to-front, side-to-side. He reaches above his head and shoves his hands down hard through the mud. He pulls himself forward, his legs like twisted ropes. He gives a sudden, violent spasm releasing himself from the sink hole. He flops face down on land beside the hole.

After these silent minutes of intense struggling, he is free and caked in mud. Exhausted.

Eventually, from the distance.

PURCHAS: Lieutenant Ross? Where are you?

ROBERT: *(Weakly.)* Here.

MACDONALD: Lieutenant Ross—

ROBERT: *(Barely audible.)* It's all right. I'm all right.

              The men reappear.

MACDONALD: What the hell?

ROBERT: Help me up.

LEVITT: Let's get out of here.

              PURCHAS and MACDONALD help ROBERT to stand. Sound of crows.

MACDONALD: Follow me, and stay close.

              In the distance again explosions and gun fire. The men fade away.

ROBERT strips off his muddy clothes as a bathtub appears on the soiled landscape.

He get in and soaks.

MRS. ROSS: *(Offstage.)* Son?

> *MRS. ROSS enters, not waiting for a response. She is carrying an empty glass.*

A mother's prerogative to visit the wounded. You look awful.

ROBERT: Thank you.

MRS. ROSS: You leave tomorrow? Suitcase packed?

ROBERT: Yes.

MRS. ROSS: They predict rain.

ROBERT: Yes.

MRS. ROSS: It's a good thing it didn't rain today. Rowena's funeral was grim enough on its own. We didn't need rain on top of it all.

> *Silence. MRS. ROSS sits on the ground by the tub.*

How is your shoulder? Did Father hurt you bad?

ROBERT: He didn't mean to.

MRS. ROSS: *(Noticing his shoulder, touching it.)* There's such a large blue mark just above your shoulder blades.

> *Smiles.*

You look as if you'd gone to sea and had yourself tattooed.

ROBERT: Yes. I could see it in the mirror.

MRS. ROSS: Do you want me to help in any way?

ROBERT: No. Thank you.

MRS. ROSS: Once, when you were a child you fell down. Skating.

ROBERT: I fell down a lot.

MRS. ROSS: Yes. But this time you were skating. Your elbows and your knees swelled up—worse than Uncle Harry with the gout.

> *She laughs.*

And your arms and thighs and your shins were simply black with bruises. Black and blue and yellow. Just like a savage painted for the wars. How alarmed we always were—every time you fell…

ROBERT: Yes.

> *MRS. ROSS breaks into uncontrollable laughter.*

MRS. ROSS: If only you'd seen yourself. Wearing those crazy skates! You were such a serious child. Everything was done with such great concentration.

> *She laughs.*

Thump! Thump! Thump! You were coming up the walk. I don't know where you'd been—but you were walking on your ankles wearing those crazy skates! You were five years old and your hair was standing straight on end.

You must've come a long, long way, that day. Your expression was so intent. I can even hear the sound of the blades as you scraped them over the bricks. Like someone sharpening knives. Still you persevered—and later you were captain of the team. Funny how most people fall down and nothing happens. Some people bruise like apples. But most people…nothing.

ROBERT: Yes.

               MRS. ROSS stands.

MRS. ROSS: You think Rowena belonged to you. Well I'm here
               to tell you, Robert, no one belongs to anyone. We're
               all cut off at birth with a knife and left at the mercy
               of strangers. You hear that? Strangers.

               *MRS. ROSS splashes ROBERT with his own bath
               water.*

               I know you're going to go away and be a soldier.
               Well—you can go to hell. I'm not responsible. I'm
               just another stranger. Birth I can give you—but life
               I cannot. I can't keep anyone alive. Not any more.

               *MRS. ROSS stares at her empty glass. She slowly
               exits. ROBERT stares off.*

Scene Eight: New Home

               *Distant explosions. Men sing, to the tune of 'Auld
               Lang Syne.'*

MEN: "We're here because we're here because
               we're here because we're here,
               we're here because we're here because
               we're here because we're here."

               *A dugout complete with a delightful collection of
               found objects: Stained-glass door, plaster angel,
               crates, stools, candles and a stove. GUY COTÉ,
               French Canadian, is repairing a small plaster sheep
               and singing "Un Canadien Errant" as he works.*

LEVITT: *(Off.)* Helloooooooo?

PURCHAS: *(Off.)* Anyone home?

               *PURCHAS, REGIS and LEVITT enter with bags.
               They notice the stained glass door.*

REGIS: Would you look at that?

PURCHAS: What the hell?

COTÉ: Attention à la porte!

LEVITT: What a marvellous piece of work.

REGIS: Who's the man in the glass?

COTÉ: That's St. Eloi. Please be careful.

LEVITT: Astonishing.

PURCHAS: I'm Purchas. This here is Levitt, and the young fella is Regis.

REGIS: Hello.

COTÉ: Guy Coté. Bienvenue. Apologies for barking at you about the door. It's just that it's a delicate piece. I took it from a church up the road. I'm rather fond of it.

LEVITT lifts the angel sculpture.

LEVITT: Are you a religious man?

COTÉ: Not in the least.

ROBERT and MACDONALD enter with bags.

ROBERT: Hello! Anyone home?

COTÉ: Attention! La porte! *(Noticing ROBERT's rank.)* Bienvenue, sir, welcome. We've been expecting you. I'm Gunner Guy Coté.

ROBERT: Second Lieutenant Robert Ross. Nice to meet you. This is Sergeant Patrick MacDonald. Would you look at this place…

COTÉ: There's not much room to spread out, I know. Lieutenant, you can put your things over here.

ROBERT: Thank you, Gunner. Where do we sleep?

COTÉ: What do you mean? Wherever you like…

ROBERT: Oh.

LEVITT spots a small cage.

LEVITT: What on earth's this?

COTÉ: That's Sergeant Rodwell's toad. You mustn't touch it. Rodwell is very protective. And he has been here for ages. Almost since the beginning. So he likes things to stay a certain way.

ROBERT: And he keeps a toad?

COTÉ: Well—he sort of keeps a lot of things. Look under that board just there.

ROBERT lifts a board covering a row of cages.

ROBERT: Birds…and is that a hedgehog? Would you look at that.

COTÉ: They've all been injured. That's his sort of hospital.

PURCHAS: Well—Rodwell's not the only one with surprises.

The men open their knapsacks. COTÉ looks in.

COTÉ: Eggs? I don't believe it!

REGIS: And cigarettes—two hundred!

PURCHAS: Canned peaches—four tins!

MACDONALD: Two tins of canned salmon!

ROBERT: Fifty candles!

PURCHAS: Four cans of chicken stew!

ROBERT: And to top it off—Nestlé's chocolate—six bars!

COTÉ: *(Disappointed.)* No wine?

MACDONALD: No, I'm afraid not.

COTÉ: Oh. Too bad. It's not the same without wine.

ROBERT: Yes, I agree. We only have—

               Reaching in sack.

               Cognac—one litre!

COTÉ: Cognac—one litre! Lieutenant—bless your heart and soul! Mon cher ami, mon bon ami, mon ami à vie!

               Takes up cognac lovingly. To LEVITT.

               What's in your sack?

LEVITT: Books.

COTÉ: Books? Maudit. What a waste of a knapsack.

MACDONALD: Maybe not. What sort of books have you brought, Levitt?

LEVITT: *(Pulling out a book.)* "Clausewitz on War."

               They stare at him.

               Well, someone has to know what he's doing.

COTÉ: Here he comes....

               SERGEANT RODWELL—dour—enters.

               This is Sergeant Rodwell—Second Lieutenant Ross—

ROBERT: Pleased to meet you.

COTÉ: And—

MACDONALD: Sergeant MacDonald.

RODWELL: Barely room to stand up all at the same time.

ROBERT: Yes, well…

RODWELL: It's going to be tight.

ROBERT: Better huddled in here then out there in the mud.

Silence.

Gentlemen, my friend Purchas here holds the key to your salvation. We've saved the best for last.

PURCHAS pulls out a package.

PURCHAS: Yes, sir. Oatmeal cookies, all the way from home!

ROBERT: Let's eat.

The men set out the food. Cognac is poured and dinner is shared. The cookies, of course, are favoured.

COTÉ: Bienvenue chez nous. Welcome to your new home.

ROBERT: Home. Interesting thought…

RODWELL: At least you're alive.

COTÉ: Don't mind Rodwell. He's just shy.

Laughter.

We look forward to your leadership, Lieutenant.

RODWELL: Maybe you can get us out of here.

ROBERT: I'll do my best.

REGIS: Coté, you've certainly made the most of it with the things you've salvaged.

COTÉ: Hard to believe you even left Canada, don't you think? Close one eye, throw dirt in the other and look around. Just like home.

LEVITT: A toast to this well appointed hole!

ROBERT: To our new home.

They clink glasses. Distant sound of bombardments. They notice but say nothing. They eat. RODWELL pulls out the toad cage and feeds the toad.

Sudden explosion nearby.

LEVITT: Take cover!

LEVITT dives quickly. No one else follows.

The initial sound is worse than the end result. LEVITT is embarrased.

May I offer anyone a peach?

COTÉ: Don't mind if I do.

LEVITT: Here you go...

ROBERT studies the cages close up.

ROBERT: Where in heavens did you find the hedgehog?

RODWELL: Under a hedge.

Laughter.

ROBERT: I suppose that means you found the bird in the sky.

RODWELL: Would that I had, Mr. Ross. No, I found him with the hedgehog. They were crouched side by side when I got them. We were all there together, actually. It was a popular hedge, just at that moment.

ROBERT: May I help you feed them?

RODWELL: If you'd like.

ROBERT: Do you work with animals back home?

RODWELL: Well, no. Not really. Actually, I draw for a living.

LEVITT: An artiste? Mercy me. I'm sorry to say I don't know much about...

RODWELL: I illustrate children's books.

MACDONALD: Fairy tales?

PURCHAS: Once upon a time…

RODWELL: There's nothing wrong with fairy tales. Sometimes, I wouldn't mind a good old-fashioned beanstalk to get me out of all this mud.

ROBERT: Or a magic potion…

RODWELL: But what I do is quite realistic. I would draw that toad the Lieutenant is holding, for instance, just as he is without embellishment. In his own right, you know, he has a good deal of character.

ROBERT: I thought it was improper to refer to animals as "he" and "she".

RODWELL: It depends how well you know them. Toad, here— I think of him as a "he". We've endured a lot together.

ROBERT: May I ask what rank he has?

RODWELL: You may. He's a Field Marshal.

              Laughter.

ROBERT: Well then, Rodwell—we must call him "sir" and have done with it.

              Laughter. Louder sound of bombardment.

LEVITT: *(To the air.)* Yes, we hear you! We're finished for the day, thank you very much.

              LEVITT remains on edge throughout the following. ROBERT takes out a note pad and begins to write.

COTÉ: J'aime les peches! I think a peach is probably the finest thing I can think of.

RODWELL: You're drunk, Guy dear…

COTÉ: Oh, I do hope that is true.

MACDONALD: *(To ROBERT.)* Writing again? You're always scribbling away.

ROBERT: I am?

MACDONALD: Yes you are. Please tell me you're not spending all this time writing your folks.

ROBERT: No. Not tonight.

> *He goes back to writing.*

COTÉ: J'aime les peches! Je les aime…

RODWELL: Enough from you.

COTÉ: Sorry.

> *REGIS begins warming up his concertina. MACDONALD reads over ROBERT's shoulder.*

MACDONALD: Who's Harris?

ROBERT: A Gunner I met on the ship coming over.

PURCHAS: What ever happened to him?

ROBERT: He should be here on this patrol but he came down with pneumonia while on the ship so he's back in England. In hospital.

MACDONALD: You mean that boy who spent all his time watching for whales? The kid from Nova Scotia?

ROBERT: We've been writing to each other.

MACDONALD: Oh.

ROBERT: I'm getting reports from the vantage point of his hospital bed.

PURCHAS: What does he write about?

ROBERT: Amusing things. About the ocean. And about whales. I keep him up to date on our progress.

MACDONALD: Did he ever see a whale after all?

ROBERT: No. I stood on whale watch with him on the ship most nights, but we never saw one. Not even once.

MACDONALD: I told him he was wasting his time. Standing out in that weather could have killed him.

ROBERT: Yes…well…

COTÉ: Young man, play us a song. The peaches have made me sad.

REGIS: I will indeed. Anything special you'd like?

COTÉ: Just don't play 'Abide With Me.'

Distant rumbles.

RODWELL takes out his sketchbook and begins to draw. COTÉ eats his peach. MACDONALD goes off. REGIS plays. LEVITT speaks over the music.

LEVITT: Clausewitz says an excess of artillery leads to a passive character in war. He says artillery must seek out great natural obstacles so that the enemy's forces must come themselves and seek their own destruction. That way, he says, the whole war can be carried out as a formal minuet…

RODWELL: A minuet! That's nice. Everybody likes to dance.

PURCHAS: I sure would like to have Cindy in my arms right now.

COTÉ: It's been so long, I don't know if I'd remember what to do.

REGIS: I danced with a girl once. Her name was Jean Louise.

ROBERT: My sister and I used to love to dance.

COTÉ: Your sister?

(l to r): Meg Roe (Rowena) and Christian Goutsis (Ross).

ROBERT: We'd steal away to the barn. I'd play the phonograph for her. And then I'd move her about in her chair.

REGIS: Her chair?

ROBERT: Yes—well, she…

> *Pulls out photograph.*

Take a look. Here she is on her birthday.

> *Men gather around ROBERT.*

RODWELL: Are those rabbits?

ROBERT: Yes, she adored them. They took over the house. For months they went everywhere with her. Every Saturday when my parents would go off to the club, Rowena and I would have our own special dance nights.

> *Around the dugout the silhouette of a barn emerges.*

ROWENA: *(Off.)* Robert, where are you?

ROBERT: We'd sneak off to the barn.

> *ROWENA enters in her wheelchair holding a handful of wildflowers.*

ROWENA: Robert, I'm ready.

ROBERT: We'd be there for hours.

> *A ladder and a cage up high appears.*

They lived high up in the loft, out of harm's way. Rowena would bring a treat for them to snack on.

> *ROBERT takes the flowers, climbs the ladder and places them in the cage.*

The rabbits became our audience.

> *More ladders, now with flickering candles, appear.*

We'd light candles all around.

And then, we'd dance.

> *Music is heard. ROWENA and ROBERT 'dance' which involves ROBERT moving the chair in co-ordinated actions. ROWENA moves her arms in beautiful time to the music. It is surprisingly smooth. ROBERT eventually lifts ROWENA out of her chair. He holds her close and continues to 'dance' with her. The men watch.*

We'd pretend we were waltzing by the lake. The rabbits would watch—the horse too—and I could swear all the creatures were smiling back at us.

RODWELL: Who does she dance with now that you're over here?

> *ROBERT stops dancing. Shaken.*

> *Without warning, an explosion close by. The barn and dance disolve back into the reality of the dugout. Things fall off shelves. Bombardment becomes deafening and blinding. Smoke fills the room. Shelves collapse. A bag of flour explodes in the room filling the air. The tin roof starts to come down.*

> *Utter darkness.*

Act Two

Scene One: Destruction

> *Explosions rip through the air. The dugout twenty minutes later. Darkness.*

RODWELL: Lieutenant—

ROBERT: Damn it. Is everyone all right?

RODWELL: Ross—

ROBERT: Where are you, Rodwell?

RODWELL: I'm on top of you, sir.

ROBERT: Can you move?

RODWELL: No sir. Something's on top of me. I think it's covered in rubble.

ROBERT: Regis?

REGIS: Yes, sir.

ROBERT: Purchas?

PURCHAS: I'm here, sir. Don't move, I'll get you out.

ROBERT: Coté? Where are you?

COTÉ: Here. We'll get you out, sir.

ROBERT: Levitt?

> *Silence.*

Can you hear me? Levitt?

LEVITT: *(Hiding.)* I don't want to come out.

RODWELL: We aren't playing hide-and-seek, damn it. Come out and help.

LEVITT: Just leave me be.

ROBERT: Levitt! Help, damn it, help.

LEVITT: All right. All right, sir, I will.

ROBERT: MacDonald? Where's MacDonald?

PURCHAS: I can't see him.

> *The men call out for MACDONALD.*

ROBERT: MacDonald? Call out if you can. Goddamn it!

LEVITT: Don't swear so much, please. I really can't bear it.

ROBERT: Will you see what you can do about getting the Sergeant off my damn back?

LEVITT: Please don't swear at me, sir.

> *LEVITT is lost, in shock. He clutches his book.*

ROBERT: What are you waiting for? Help us.

LEVITT: I'm looking for somewhere to put down my book.

PURCHAS: Give it to me. Then you can help me pull this stuff away.

> *LEVITT and PURCHAS begin to clear.*

LEVITT: I said I would help, didn't I? Just leave me be.

RODWELL: Slow down. You're hurting me.

> *RODWELL and ROBERT are freed. The men attempt to restore order.*

LEVITT: Would you please not put those things there? I'm doing my best to get this place in order. You just keep knocking everything down and putting equipment where it doesn't belong! And leave my books alone!

REGIS: Fine. I'm sorry.

PURCHAS: Since when did you get so concerned about where things went? What's wrong with you?

LEVITT: *(Lost.)* I don't know.

> *Men continue searching for MACDONALD while also clearing the dugout.*

Stop it! Stop it! You're doing it again! You're messing everything up!

> *RODWELL strikes LEVITT in the face.*

RODWELL: Now shut up and help.

ROBERT: My God. Where's MacDonald? Where could he be?

> *They quickly toss debris aside. Nobody notices that another figure has entered and joined in the searching.*

MACDONALD: Who are we looking for?

ROBERT: MacDonald?!?! We were looking for you—damn it—YOU! Fool!

MACDONALD: I'm sorry, sir. I went to relieve myself and got caught between the dugout and the trench. I didn't dare move.

ROBERT: Next time, stay in your place so we know where you are.

MACDONALD: *(Smiling.)* Yes, sir. I will.

COTÉ: Look.

> *COTÉ holds up a piece of broken stained glass. RODWELL holds up toad.*

RODWELL: Only one survivor. Toad.

            *RODWELL places toad in a bucket. COTÉ covers it
            with his broken glass.*

            Large explosion.

            *Other men appear on the ruined landscape,
            wandering and digging out men. LEVITT drifts
            about—full shock. Robert bumps into him.*

ROBERT: Levitt? How are you feeling?

LEVITT: The air, sir. The air.

ROBERT: What, Levitt?

LEVITT: The air. The air. Can't breathe.

            LEATHER approaches ROBERT.

LEATHER: You there. I'm looking for Second Lieutenant Ross.

ROBERT: I am Ross, sir.

LEATHER: Good to meet you.

ROBERT: Sir, we've met before. On the ship over from
            Canada.

LEATHER: Right. How many of your men down?

ROBERT: I haven't been able to tally that yet, sir.

LEATHER: Fine. Fine. Listen to me. The fields are ripped up,
            a mess. We're going to have to lay down new gun
            beds.

ROBERT: What, sir?

LEATHER: Just listen. Take anyone left standing, Lieutenant.
            Look.

            LEATHER studies a map with ROBERT.

            The gun beds will have to be put in here and there.

ROBERT: There, sir? But, sir—that's at the far edge of the crater, directly at the German lines.

LEATHER: Just so. We don't have a choice. And you only have these remaining men till I can request more. I'm putting you in charge. Don't mess this up.

ROBERT: Yes, sir.

LEATHER: Good boy. Just let them know you're in command. They should be fine once you get them into action.

> *Calling out.*

Soldiers, over here.

> *The men gather.*

Lieutenant Ross is leading the next charge. We need to move quickly and put down new gun beds. Gather your things and follow the Lieutenant. You leave immediately.

> *The men gather the required equipment. LEVITT walks directly to LEATHER and stares at him. After an awkward moment LEATHER departs abruptly.*

ROBERT: Levitt?

LEVITT: It's not safe out here.

ROBERT: Levitt. Are you up for this?

LEVITT: Let's go hide somewhere—where it's safe.

ROBERT: Levitt…listen to me…

LEVITT: Somewhere quiet.

ROBERT: I need you to listen to me, Levitt.

> *Stalling while he considers.*

I have a special task for you. Stay back here and

make sure tea is ready when we return. Can you
do that? It's very important.

LEVITT: Tea? Yes, Lieutenant.

ROBERT: Very good, Levitt.

LEVITT: I can have tea ready. Everything will be neat. Tidy.
Clean. Safe.

ROBERT: Soldiers! Move out.

*ROBERT leads the other men onwards, leaving
LEVITT all alone to wander.*

LEVITT: Fresh air.

Scene Two: The Crater

Sunrise. Battle sounds continue.

The men appear on an elevated area, very high up.

*They carry shovels, ladders, and the wooden boxes
that hold the mortars and ammunition. They are
looking down into a large hole.*

PURCHAS: Would you look at that.

MACDONALD: That is one massive crater.

REGIS: My mother wouldn't want me to go any further
than this.

ROBERT: Lower the ladders. *(The men do so.)* Where's home,
Regis?

REGIS: Regina. *(In awe.)* Honest, sir! This is worse than
the cyclone of 1912. It's worse than the Wascana
flood!

ROBERT: We'll cross the crater and cut gun beds about ten
feet below the opposite lip. Do you see that thing
that looks like a ski pole?

(l to r): Kevin K. James (Macdonald), Christian Goutsis (Ross), Stafford Perry (Regis), Paul Anthony (Purchas), Hrothgar Mathews (Soldier) and Rachael V. Johnston (Soldier).

RODWELL: Yes, sir.

ROBERT: We'll head for that first.

RODWELL: Yes, sir.

ROBERT: Follow Sergeant Rodwell's signals.

MEN: Yes, sir.

> *ROBERT climbs down. He gives the sign to RODWELL who then alerts the men. They start down the crater. Mortars are lowered on ropes.*
>
> *MACDONALD comes up to what turns out to be a ski pole.*

MACDONALD: Well—of all things. It *is* a ski pole.

COTÉ: How in the hell did it get here?

> *MACDONALD starts miming skiing with the pole, messing around. ROBERT takes out a notebook and makes some calculations.*
>
> *For the first time today silence descends. The men notice this one by one.*

PURCHAS: What's going on? It's too quiet.

MACDONALD: I don't suppose the Germans are taking a break.

ROBERT: Sit tight. It doesn't necessarily mean anything.

> *Silence.*

COTÉ: Lieutenant?

ROBERT: What, Coté?

COTÉ: Sir—

> *COTÉ points at the side of the crater they climbed down. A low cloud of yellow gas starts to pour over the lip of the crater. ROBERT gets his gas mask out.*

(l to r): Andrew McNee (Coté), Christian Goutsis (Ross), Jordan Schartner (Rodwell),
Hrothgar Mathews (Soldier) and Erin Wells (Soldier).

REGIS: What is it? What is it?

ROBERT: Quickly, men. Put on your masks.

                The men just stare at him.

                Put on your masks. Immediately!

PURCHAS: I can't, sir.

ROBERT: What the hell do you mean?

                Looks at others.

                Put your masks on!

REGIS: I *can't* either, sir. I wasn't given one.

ROBERT: Every man is issued a mask.

COTÉ: No, sir. It's not true.

ROBERT: What are you talking about?

MACDONALD: I left mine in the dugout. Damn it.

                MACDONALD tries to wrest ROBERT's mask from him. ROBERT pulls out his gun.

ROBERT: Back off or I'll fire, MacDonald.

RODWELL: Back off!

ROBERT: Listen you sons-of-bitches! Do exactly what I say. Now, if you all want to live, you have about twenty seconds. Get out your handkerchiefs...

MACDONALD: He's insane!

                MACDONALD starts to climb back out to escape — ROBERT shoots towards him — deliberately missing. MACDONALD falls, injuring himself.

RODWELL: I don't have a handkerchief.

ROBERT: Then tear the tails off your goddamned shirts!

> *Grumbling, they start tearing. ROBERT throws his mask to REGIS and points to MACDONALD.*

Put that over his face.

> *REGIS does.*

REGIS: What are we s'posed to do?

PURCHAS: These won't save us. Not if it's chlorine.

ROBERT: Piss on them.

COTÉ: Huh?

ROBERT: Piss on them!!!!

> *Everyone begins. Too nervous, COTÉ panics.*

COTÉ: Cher Jésus, laisse moi pisser....

ROBERT: Damn you! Give it to me!

> *ROBERT takes COTÉ's cloth and urinates on it.*

Put it over your face. All you others do the same.
Lie down flat with your face in your hands.

> *They look at him, dumbfounded.*

Do it!!!

> *They do so. ROBERT urinates what he can onto his own handkerchief and covers his face. They all lie down, as instructed.*

> *They wait.*

> *The fog of gas, which has been pouring down the side of the crater, covers them completely.*

> *ROWENA appears in her wheelchair and rolls through the gas and the men, searching. She finds*

ROBERT. He is surprised to see her. ROWENA smiles. They hold hands for a moment.

It begins to snow.

ROWENA disappears.

Eventually, the gas clears. The snow covers the men. They appear as if under a perfect blanket.

Silence.

ROBERT: Soldiers? Men? Call out.

MEN: Yes, sir.

ROBERT: Rodwell?

RODWELL: Yes, sir?

ROBERT: We should be safe, now. I'm going to roll over. I don't want anybody to move just yet.

RODWELL: Yes, sir.

> *ROBERT eases himself into a sitting position. He becomes the only brown image in the field.*

ROBERT: Who would have thought that something I learned in school would come in handy? Chemistry class. Piss neutralizes chlorine. Piss. Who would have thought?

> *He laughs. The men laugh.*

RODWELL: Thank you sir, thank you.

PURCHAS: Thank you, sir.

> *All the men begin to murmur 'thank you.'*

> *ROBERT takes his accomplishment in. Then he spots something across the crater and freezes in place.*

ROBERT: Don't move. There's somebody up there. A German. Keep your heads down.

Very slowly ROBERT draws his gun. He holds it for the [unseen] German to see, but does not point it at him.

Rodwell? There's only one and I don't think he has a gun. Try rolling over. I've got him covered.

RODWELL rolls over.

He's indicating for you to get up. Stand right up. He isn't going to shoot.

RODWELL stands.

RODWELL: Now what?

ROBERT: Go to the top. Back the way we came. Just go. But go slowly. Don't alarm him.

RODWELL climbs back up, out of the crater.

Whatever his reasons are—he wants us to go free. I want everyone to join Rodwell. Don't stop and don't look back. Keep your hands in the air, so he'll know you're not armed. Maybe he's crazy but he isn't going to kill us.

The men climb out of the crater. They hide out of sight. MACDONALD has not moved.

MacDonald. Can you crawl back up? It's safe to take your mask off now. Can't you hear me? MacDonald!

ROBERT turns him over. Surprised.

Dead.

ROBERT begins to climb nervously—he has no protection. Every step forward he makes, he falls back two. He is almost to the top.

RODWELL: *(Seeing the [unseen] German move, he yells out.)* Sir—

> *ROBERT turns quickly and without hesitation shoots the [unseen] German. A startled cry is heard from the German.*

PURCHAS: Got him!

> *RODWELL joins ROBERT down in the crater.*

RODWELL: Let's pack up and get out of here.

> *Other men come back into the crater to pack up.*

> *After catching his breath, ROBERT looks through the field glasses.*

ROBERT: His hands are nowhere near his gun. He was only reaching for his binoculars.

> *ROBERT looks more.*

He had a Mauser rifle with him. He could have killed us all. Why?

COTÉ: C'est bizarre. C'est…fou. Que c'est qu'on fait ici? Que c'est qui ce passé? Le monde est…fou. C'est tut-fou.

ROBERT: Yes. Strange.

> *CAPTAIN LEATHER appears at the top of the crater wearing a gas mask. He climbs into the crater and then takes off the mask.*

> *LEATHER looks directly at RODWELL.*

LEATHER: Lieutenant Ross, what are you wasting all this time for? You've achieved nothing.

ROBERT: Sir…I am Ross.

LEATHER: Ah, yes. Just so. Well…a waste of time.

> *Sound of an aeroplane going by. LEATHER notices.*

Free as a bird...

LEATHER wanders off.

PURCHAS: You saved our lives. Thank you Lieutenant. Let's go home.

ROBERT: Home.

No one can speak. ROBERT stares in the direction of the dead German. The men move off.

Scene Three: Sickness

A hospital in London. Beds are filled with wounded soldiers. One or two patients have visitors. MARIAN, a British nurse, tends to a patient. NURSE JACKIE enters with a cablegram.

JACKIE: Good morning, Marian.

MARIAN: Good morning, Jackie.

JACKIE: This just came in. You won't like it.

MARIAN: Not more?

JACKIE: I'm afraid so.

MARIAN: But we are full as it is.

JACKIE: Yes, I know. Perhaps we can add beds in the hall?

MARIAN: It's too much to bear. When do they say?

JACKIE: In two days.

MARIAN: We'll find room. Of course, we will find room.

A SOLDIER: Nurse?

JACKIE: Yes, Sergeant.

JACKIE crosses to the bed of the soldier who

called out as ROBERT, PURCHAS, COTÉ, and RODWELL enter.

PURCHAS: Why do all hospitals smell the same?

RODWELL: Still—I'd take this place over the mud back in France any day.

MARIAN approaches.

MARIAN: Good day, Gentlemen.

ROBERT: Hello, miss. We're looking for Private Harris.

MARIAN: Yes, sir. *(Points to HARRIS's' bed.)*

ROBERT: Miss, could you tell me how he is?

MARIAN: He's had pneumonia for some time now. One day he seems to be beating it, the next day he seems even worse. Today he's somewhere in between, sir.

ROBERT: I see.

MARIAN: It's lovely of you to visit. Especially when…

ROBERT: When?

MARIAN: When someone is terribly ill.

ROBERT: Right….

MARIAN: No one should…

ROBERT: Yes?

MARIAN: Die alone, sir.

Silence.

Where did you lads come from then?

COTÉ: France. We're on leave for a week.

RODWELL: It's been two months now without a free day.

MARIAN: Well then, welcome to London. You're very generous. Not many people would spend their free time—

ROBERT: Well, he's a friend.

MARIAN: We've sent cablegrams to his family, but no word back.

PURCHAS: It's a shame to think he came all this way and he's not seen any battle.

MARIAN: If I may say so, maybe he's the fortunate one.

ROBERT: Maybe.

The men move to HARRIS. HARRIS wears his scarf. After a time, he opens his eyes and smiles. His breathing is laboured.

HARRIS: I knew it.

ROBERT: I promised.

HARRIS: I know.

ROBERT: Do you remember Purchas from the ship?

PURCHAS: Hello again. You haven't missed much.

ROBERT: And this is Gunner Coté and Sergeant Rodwell.

COTÉ: Good to meet you, Harris.

HARRIS: Good to meet you too, soldier.

PURCHAS: But we've forgotten to introduce our Field Marshal.

RODWELL pulls out toad from a small can.

HARRIS: He survived the gas attack!

RODWELL: Thanks to some stained glass, and a bucket full of water. Would you do me a favour?

HARRIS: Yes, Sergeant.

RODWELL: Would you look after the Field Marshal for me?

HARRIS: Certainly.

RODWELL: He's much better off here in England.

COTÉ: He's no longer in a country where his legs are in danger of being eaten.

HARRIS: Thank you, I'll take great care. But I'm anxious to join you all in France. Please, catch me up on everything.

HARRIS has a coughing fit.

PURCHAS: Ross, we'll leave you two for a bit.

COTÉ: Yes. Good idea.

RODWELL: We'll come back in a few hours.

ROBERT: All right. Go and enjoy London.

RODWELL, COTÉ and PURCHAS go out.

It's good to see you.

HARRIS: I've missed you.

ROBERT: Oh. Yes.

Silence.

Thank you for your letters. You've kept me busy resplying to all your...

HARRIS: Well, I want to know everything.

ROBERT: I've done my best.

HARRIS: Anything new from your parents?

ROBERT: Another letter just arrived from them. I haven't been able to open it.

HARRIS: But Robert—

ROBERT: I know, I know. It's difficult. Reading vacant letters.
             All these words going back and forth and nothing
             truly being said.

HARRIS: But Robert—

             Silence.

ROBERT: How are you holding up in this place?

HARRIS: Hard to...breathe...sometimes...

ROBERT: And how do you cope with being inside all the
             time?

HARRIS: Oh, it's not bad at all. I go out quite often.

ROBERT: You do?

HARRIS: Today I swam with a pod of whales.

ROBERT: You swam...with whales?

HARRIS: The water was a bit cold but it was worth every
             minute of it.

ROBERT: You swam with whales?

HARRIS: Oh, yes. You must come with me sometime. Guess
             what I discovered? Under water you can hear them
             sing.

ROBERT: Whales...sing? I don't imagine that whales make
             any sound at all, Harris.

HARRIS: Oh yes—they do. They sing ever so loudly.

             HARRIS makes the sound of a whale singing.

             And sometimes the whales beach themselves and
             then the fishermen come in boats and slaughter
             them...

             After a moment, drifting.

Sometimes I lie offshore and let myself be carried in by tides that wash up the sand...and the sand...

ROBERT: What about the sand?

HARRIS: ...the sand is red. I float that way sometimes for hours, just to get the feel of landfall—sort of the way a million years ago or more we came ashore ourselves as fish or—

Holding up toad bucket.

toads or whatever we were—floating through the slaughter.

ROBERT: You'd make a ridiculous looking toad. Stick to being a soldier.

HARRIS: No. Believe me.

ROBERT: All right, all right.

HARRIS: You must believe me. Everyone who's born has come from the sea. We're all creatures of the ocean—walking on land.

ROBERT imitates the whale noises he heard HARRIS attempt. HARRIS joins in. Their whale sounds and eventual laughter fill the room. MARIAN notices this and smiles.

ROBERT: Weren't you afraid, swimming around with the whales that way?

HARRIS: Not at all. I can take care of myself. And I'm not afraid now. Are you?

ROBERT: I don't think I am. Imagine that.

HARRIS: I think that your sister is proud of you.

ROBERT: What do you mean?

HARRIS: I know she's not with us, but she is watching over you.

Silence.

ROBERT: Do you think so?

HARRIS: Yes, I really do.

ROBERT: There's something I haven't told you. About my sister. *(Silence.)* How she died.

HARRIS: What do you mean?

ROBERT: She died trying to reach her rabbits. High up in the loft.

HARRIS: Oh.

ROBERT: I was supposed to be watching her that night. And I wasn't there. I had promised her and so she was waiting to dance with me. Like we always did.

HARRIS: Robert…

ROBERT: But that night I wasn't thinking of her. I was in my room…I was…. I wasn't thinking of her at all. By the time I got to the barn, she was lying lifeless on the ground. She had tried to climb up to the loft to feed the rabbits. Those damn rabbits. And I was the one who gave them to her. She was trying to feed them, as I always did. But because I wasn't there to…

HARRIS: It's not your fault.

ROBERT: I'm not sure of that. I told her I would be there. I promised. And I let that happen.

Silence.

She haunts me.

HARRIS: I know.

ROBERT: Everything haunts me.

Silence.

HARRIS: I know. That's why you need me. To teach you. I
             need to teach you how to swim with whales. It's
             much easier than you think. You'll be swimming
             like a fish before you know it. I'll be your guide.

             *HARRIS places his hand on ROBERT's hand. They
             share a quiet moment. Suddenly, MARIAN and the
             patient she is with begin to laugh loudly.*

MARIAN: Excuse me everyone. Please excuse me.

HARRIS: No, no. Please don't stop laughing. It reminds
             me of down home. Are there rules here against
             laughter?

MARIAN: No, of course not.

ROBERT: It's a nice thing to hear.

HARRIS: Please, carry on.

ROBERT: Maybe it will be contagious.

MARIAN: That's a lovely idea... The Captain and I were
             just talking about life after the war. Such grand
             nonsense.

ROBERT: Like what?

MARIAN: Family picnics. Sunday night dinners at home.
             Staying up till the sun rises. Peace. Nonsense.

             *Silence. ROBERT notices that HARRIS has drifted
             off to sleep.*

ROBERT: He's not doing as well as.... His letters didn't
             always make perfect sense, but I thought he was
             just fooling with me. Now, I'm not.... Oh, please
             excuse me. I should have properly introduced
             myself. I'm Second Lieutenant Robert Ross.

MARIAN: Very nice to meet you, sir.

ROBERT: And your name?

MARIAN: My name? Nurse Alexander.

ROBERT: Do you have a first name?

MARIAN: Yes, sir.

ROBERT: Well, may I ask what it is?

MARIAN: Marian, sir.

ROBERT: I'm not all that comfortable with titles. May I call you Marian?

MARIAN: Of course. Thank you, sir.

ROBERT: Thank you, Marian. Call me Robert, if you like.

MARIAN: Yes, sir. Where are you from?

ROBERT: Canada.

MARIAN: Canada! Of course, I should have guessed that. I've never been. All that land. Unspoiled country. One day I'd like to visit. After the war.

ROBERT: I hope you do.

MARIAN: May I ask you a question?

ROBERT: Yes. Of course.

MARIAN: How do you find it? The war. I only see it from inside this room. I can't, obviously, ask the people in here. How is it, I mean how is it really, out there on the fields?

ROBERT: Oh….

MARIAN: Forgive me, I—

ROBERT: Deafening. The unrelenting sound of mortar fire. Horse cries. It's dreadful. It's deafening.

MARIAN: So it really is as dreadful as I've been hearing then…

ROBERT: Worse.

MARIAN: Is there any light?

ROBERT: Light? Well…the men. And the odd bottle of cognac.

MARIAN: Cognac?

ROBERT: It's not a full time activity or anything.

MARIAN: I should hope not.

             They are laughing.

             I hear the grass is all but gone in France. Do you ever get used to the mud?

ROBERT: No. Never. And we keep losing horses. They drown in the mud.

MARIAN: Drown? Oh dear. Well…

TAFFLER: Nurse? Can I please have a glass of water?

MARIAN: Please excuse me, Lieutenant. Nurse? Can you please bring Captain Taffler a glass of water?

             JACKIE nods and goes off.

ROBERT: Captain Taffler? From Canada?

MARIAN: Why, yes indeed. Do you know him?

ROBERT: Yes, I do. He's a hero back home. What are the chances? I must go over.

MARIAN: Well… He's—

             ROBERT starts towards the bed.

             Oh, dear…

             She follows ROBERT, trying to stop him. He reaches the bed.

ROBERT: Captain Taffler.

TAFFLER: Yes?

ROBERT: Taffler, what a coincidence—

              TAFFLER's torso is heavily bandaged—both arms
              have been amputated. The two men stare at each
              other.

              Oh... Captain.

TAFFLER: Lieutenant Ross, isn't it?

ROBERT: Yes, Captain.

TAFFLER: Well, sit down.

              Silence. ROBERT stays standing.

              I'd offer you a drink if I could...

ROBERT: Thank you.

              He does not move.

TAFFLER: I guess you'd have to do the pouring...

ROBERT: Yes. Right.

              Silence.

TAFFLER: I suspect my baseball days are over.

ROBERT: Right.

TAFFLER: What brings you to the hospital?

ROBERT: A friend. I'm visiting a friend.

TAFFLER: I see.

ROBERT: Sir—

TAFFFLER: Yes?

Large silence. JACKIE enters with water. From another bed a soldier calls out.

A SOLDIER: Nurse—

JACKIE moves to the other soldier, passing the glass to ROBERT on the way.

ROBERT: Oh.

He helps TAFFLER to drink. It is extremely awkward. Two or three silent attempts conclude with ROBERT dropping the glass on the floor.

Please excuse me—

He backs out of the room, distressed.

TAFFLER: Don't go—Ross—Please—

ROBERT runs out. TAFFLER starts to sob. It turns into a scream.

MARIAN: Captain—Jackie, come quick. Bring morphine.

TAFFLER continues to scream and struggle to free himself of his bandages. JACKIE prepares morphine.

Scene Four: Church

Two worlds simultaneously: ROBERT enters from within the hospital. He tries to catch his breath. Moments later MR. and MRS. ROSS emerge from within a church. From inside we hear a congregation sing.

ALL: "All people that on earth do dwell,
               Sing to the Lord with cheerful voice.
               Him serve with mirth, his praise forth tell.
               Come ye before him and rejoice."

MR. ROSS: But—we can't just run out of the church like that.

MRS. ROSS: I can. With all that sitting and standing and kneeling, who will notice? Besides, why should it matter? Leave me be a moment.

She drinks from a flask.

I was afraid I was going to scream. I do not understand. I don't. I won't. I can't. Why is this happening to us? What does it mean—to kill your children? Kill them and then…go in there and sing about it! They promised us Christmas. Now look at it: Easter. And no one's coming home. They promised us Christmas! All those young men in there about to leave—smiling at their parents. Thank God and Jesus, Robert didn't smile at me before he left—I couldn't have borne it.

MR. ROSS: I know, dear.

MRS. ROSS pulls out a letter.

MRS. ROSS: Please post this. I wasn't sure that I was going to send it. But after that display in there, I'm certain that Robert needs to know what we're going through. He needs to understand what it's like to be the family left behind.

MR. ROSS: But he knows.

MRS. ROSS: If he knows, then why does he never write us about it? I'm sorry, but he has to hear everything. I can't keep it to myself any longer.

Silence.

The war to end all wars. I hope they're right.

MARIAN enters from within the hospital.

MARIAN: There you are Lieutenant.

ROBERT: Why do these things happen? I don't understand.

MARIAN: No one understands.

ROBERT: It's just that Captain Taffler's a…

MARIAN: I know.

ROBERT: I'm sorry for taking you away. You're awfully kind.

MARIAN: For a brief respite…I should thank you.

                 Looking for his handkerchief, ROBERT finds the letter in his pocket.

ROBERT: Oh. Take a look at this, would you.

                 ROBERT opens the letter. He hands the letter to MARIAN.

                 Go ahead and read it.

MARIAN: A letter from your mother? That's lovely, but I don't know that I—

ROBERT: Please. Read it aloud.

MARIAN: All right then. "Dear Robert, I have so much to share with you. I continue to support the troops on our weekly send off for the young men. Father has been busy with the business—you know how he is. We are forever proud of you. Do not worry about us—"

ROBERT: It's all made up. My father writes them and he pretends they're from her. My father's very protective. And resourceful. He's even mastered her signature.

MARIAN: How do you know?

ROBERT: I just do. But to be honest, I'm not any better. I hardly mention anything I witness over here in my letters. How can I possibly describe any of this?

MRS. ROSS: Let's go back in.

ROBERT: Let's go back in.

> *MRS. ROSS stumbles. MR. ROSS goes to her. She brushes him off.*

MRS. ROSS: If I fall down— I fall down.

> *MRS. ROSS exits. MARIAN follows. MR. ROSS and ROBERT both rip up their letters.*

Scene Five: Death

> *Five days later. Hospital again. MARIAN sits at TAFFLER's bed. She is reading from a newspaper.*

MARIAN: It says here: "they are now being afforded the same rights granted to women in Manitoba only two months ago. The suffrage movement has made its way west thereby allowing women of Alberta the right to vote." Of all things….

> *ROBERT enters carrying flowers, in fine spirits.*

JACKIE: Good morning, Lieutenant. We look forward to your daily visits.

ROBERT: You can count on me.

JACKIE: Yes, sir, we certainly can.

ROBERT: Good day, Marian! Hello, Captain Taffler.

TAFFLER: Hello, Ross.

ROBERT: Marian, these are for you.

> *He hands her the flowers.*

MARIAN: Oh. How beautiful. Thank you.

ROBERT: They're poppies. Covent Garden was busy today. I hate to say it, but this will be my last day visiting. My leave is up.

MARIAN: Lieutenant—

ROBERT: I will miss London and—

MARIAN: Lieutenant. It doesn't seem fair somehow.

ROBERT: Fair?

MARIAN: Private Harris went in the night.

ROBERT: He went?

ROBERT moves towards HARRIS' bed.

MARIAN: I'm so sorry. He just slid away. I don't think he could hold on any longer. At least you had this week together.

Silence.

If words could heal...if kindness could cure... Harris would be alive and with you today.

ROBERT sits on the empty bed.

ROBERT: So swift...

JACKIE brings over a canvas-covered box.

JACKIE: We thought you might take care of these.

ROBERT: These...

JACKIE: Yes. His...ashes.

ROBERT: His...

MARIAN: There's no one else....

ROBERT: Of course.

MARIAN: And—

MARIAN brings out HARRIS's scarf.

—his scarf.

ROBERT: My scarf.

MARIAN: Oh, Lieutenant Ross.

JACKIE: We are sorry, sir.

ROBERT: Harris. Turned to ash. It's all too quick. What will I
                do with this?

MARIAN: What would you like to do?

ROBERT: I don't know. I can't take them back to France with
                me.

MARIAN: Well...we could scatter them.

ROBERT: We could? Where?

MARIAN: Where would he like to be, do you think?

                *As ROBERT realizes, the sound of a rushing river
                fills the air.*

                *Gentle transition to the water's edge. PURCHAS,
                RODWELL, and COTÉ join MARIAN and
                ROBERT. They stand together and look out to the
                river.*

ROBERT: Gentlemen, as this is not a military funeral, just a
                burial at sea, may I suggest we take off our caps?

PURCHAS: Yes, sir.

                *They do. ROBERT places the scarf around his
                neck.*

ROBERT: I don't know what to say. I've never seen this done
                before.

MARIAN: Say anything. He can hear you.

                MARIAN takes his hand.

ROBERT: Harris, this river will take you out away from the
                city, to the channel, and then out to the ocean. I
                know you will find the way. Be well. And go in

peace, my good friend. And sing with the whales.

As ROBERT scatters the ashes into the water, the sound of whale song fills the air.

Scene Six: Something Explodes

France. Explosions. Men everywhere—exhausted and barely alive showing signs of having endured intense fighting and limited sleep. Two men pass by with a wounded soldier on a stretcher.

Sound of horse cries.

[Horses are fenced in just out of sight offstage.]

CAPTAIN LEATHER appears and speaks to men offstage.

LEATHER: Feeding the damn horses again? Don't you have anything better to do? Just leave them. Leave them you stupid fools.

Two soldiers enter with buckets.

SOLDIER 1:   Yes, sir. I'm sorry, sir.

SOLDIER 2:   Just trying to calm them down, sir.

LEATHER: Try leaving them alone.

SOLDIER 1:   Yes, sir.

SOLDIER 2:   Sorry, sir.

RODWELL comes over to ROBERT and COTÉ, with his bags.

ROBERT: Did you see that? He's not making sense anymore—he's making us all—

RODWELL: Ross. I've been told to lead the next charge with my company.

ROBERT: Forward?

ROWELL: Yes. Directly into all this mess.

ROBERT: No. Tell them you can't—tell them you—

RODWELL: Those are my orders. Nothing I can do.

ROBERT: But that can't possibly make sense. No one is coming back alive from the—

RODWELL: Yes. I know.

ROBERT: What can we do? We're helpless here. We're losing all our men.

RODWELL: Coté. Would you help me out? See that this makes it back home? It's for my daughter.

                RODWELL hands COTÉ a letter.

COTÉ: Rodwell? What are you talking about—

RODWELL: Just do it for me. Please.

COTÉ: Of course I will.

ROBERT: If anyone can survive it up there Rodwell, you can.

RODWELL: That's probably true.

ROBERT: We'll meet up soon.

RODWELL: Right.

COTÉ: Hurry back.

                They shake his hand. RODWELL goes. The men watch him leave.

ROBERT: Coté?

COTÉ: Listowel?

ROBERT: What?

COTÉ: Listowel, Ontario.

ROBERT: Never heard of it.

COTÉ: *(Reading RODWELL's letter.)* "To my daughter, Laurine.
Love your Mother.
Make your prayers against despair.
I am alive in everything you touch.
Touch these pages and you have me in your fingertips. We survive in one another.
I am your Father always.
Everything lives forever.
Every…"

> *He stops reading. ROBERT takes the letter from him.*

ROBERT: "Everything lives forever.
Believe it.
Nothing dies."
Nothing dies?!

> *Explosion. Horses panic.*

How long is this going to go on?

COTÉ: Maudit. We've been at this one for more days than I can count.

ROBERT: It's one thing to force men to be here, but the horses don't have a choice. Fenced in like that. No one's protecting them.

COTÉ: No one's protecting anyone.

> *Huge explosion. COTÉ runs off. LEATHER enters.*

ROBERT: How much more can we take, sir? I'm living on chocolate bars and tea.

LEATHER: I'm living off rum myself.

ROBERT: I've had eight hours sleep in the last three days.

LEATHER: That much? In war, Lieutenant, these are simply the facts of life.

ROBERT: It feels more like a fact of death.

LEATHER starts to go.

Sir—

LEATHER: What is it, Lieutenant?

ROBERT: I would like to be allowed to make a strategic retreat with the horses. To keep them alive.

LEATHER: What a cowardly idea!

ROBERT: Sir…not for my sake. For theirs.

LEATHER: What would that look like? Having them retreat? We should never live it down. No, Lieutenant. You may not.

ROBERT: Sir—if we lose them none of the ammunition that we have brought up, none of it, will reach our replacements. And the wounded won't have a chance in hell of getting out. I'm thinking of our men!

LEATHER: I said no, Lieutenant. The horses stay—and so do you. That's an order.

LEATHER joins a gathering of men chatting and drinking.

More explosions and horse screams.

ROBERT looks wildly around and spots PURCHAS.

ROBERT: Purchas! The horses are going to die if we don't get them out of here.

PURCHAS: I know. So why don't you talk to Captain Leather about it?

ROBERT: I just did. He won't hear of it. Will you help me?

PURCHAS: Help you?

ROBERT: We should let the horses out and run them to safety.

PURCHAS: Go against orders?

ROBERT: All this life is at stake!

PURCHAS: But Captain Leather?

ROBERT: It can't be called disobedience to save these animals, for God's sake. They'll be needed half an hour after this noise finally stops. But if we stay here, they'll be killed. Purchas, please help me.

PURCHAS: Do you know what you're doing?

ROBERT: Yes, I know what I'm doing.

PURCHAS: Then lead on…

               They exit. Explosions and animal cries intensify. LEATHER notices. He shouts off.

LEATHER: What the hell are you up to? Shut those goddamn gates! Lieutenant! Gunner!

ROBERT: *(Offstage.)* The horses will be safer!

LEATHER: You two—stop them. Shut those gates.

               Two SOLDIERS exit towards ROBERT and PURCHAS.

               Lieutenant, you're disobeying my direct orders.

PURCHAS: *(Entering.)* Sir! I think you should listen to Ross. With all due respect, sir, I think he knows what he's saying!

ROBERT: *(Entering.)* Sir, if we save our horses we save ourselves!

LEATHER: *(Grabs ROBERT and throws him down.)* Who the hell do you think you are, Lieutenant? The only reason you are an officer in this war is because of your surname. You get that, don't you? You don't deserve to be called Lieutenant. A coward like you. Coward! I'm sending you out with the next charge. Get ready to leave.

                An airplane attack above. LEATHER and the other men rush off to take cover. Intense horses.

PURCHAS: Even if we opened the gates they won't move.

ROBERT: They're terrified. We'll have to force them out.

                As ROBERT and PURCHAS go towards the offstage horses, the two soldiers return and block their way.

SOLDIER 1:   *(Calling.)* Captain Leather.

SOLDIER 2:   Come quick.

SOLDIER 1:   Ross is opening the gates again.

                LEATHER runs on. He pulls out his revolver.

LEATHER: Stop right now. Let the horses alone!

PURCHAS: Ross is right!

                LEATHER shoots. After a moment, PURCHAS falls to the ground, dead.

LEATHER: Traitors! How dare you—

ROBERT: Noooooo !!!!!

                Explosion.

                Something snaps inside ROBERT. Now he is fury and rage.

If an animal had done this—if an animal had done this—we would call it mad and shoot it!

ROBERT draws his gun.

LEATHER laughs.

ROBERT shoots LEATHER dead.

The two SOLDIERS charge ROBERT.

He shoots both of them dead.

ROBERT turns to unseen horses.

Run, horses, run!

Pounding hooves.

White light pours in from offstage where the horses were held.

ROBERT is in the center of many escaping horses. A final explosion plunges everything into darkness.

All that can be heard are pounding hooves.

Scene Seven: Fire

Interior of a barn.

ROBERT sits on his haunches, exhausted. His pistol hangs down from his fingers. He is in rough shape. His uniform is in tatters. A few horses snort quietly.

ROBERT tears the lapels from his uniform. He discovers the photograph of his sister in his pocket. He studies it.

ROBERT: Sleep now, Rowena.

He rips it up into many pieces.

Through the cracks between the boards we see MAJOR MICKLE and a band of SOLDIERS enter warily. The voices of the men are eerily distorted—

we hear them from ROBERT's point of view now —
distant and disconnected.

MICKLE: We know you're in the barn, Lieutenant Ross. We know what you've done.

SOLDIER 3:   You've led us on quite the chase.

SOLDIER 4:   But we're here now. Let the horses out.

SOLDIER 5:   Throw down your weapon.

MICKLE: And we will take your surrender into account at your hearing.

ROBERT: We are not going back.

MICKLE: Who's in there with him?

SOLDIER 4:   Don't know, sir. I don't know. The report was that he was alone.

MICKLE: What does he mean by 'we' then? Who's in there?

SOLDIER 3:   Can't see. I think he might just mean the horses.

MICKLE: I'm not so sure. Identify yourselves in there! If you won't come out, we have no choice but to smoke you out.

               ROBERT fires a shot through the boards.

               I'm giving you one last chance.

               ROBERT fires again.

ROBERT: We will not be taken. Back off and let us retreat.

MICKLE: Give the signal to start the fire.

SOLDIER 4:   You have no way out. Do you hear us in there?

SOLDIER 3:   All of you.

SOLDIER 5:   Cowards!

SOLDIER 6:   We'll smoke you men out!

MICKLE: Don't any of you men in there listen to Lieutenant Ross. He's a traitor.

SOLDIER 5:   Come out now.

SOLDIER 3:   There's no escape.

SOLDIER 4:   The horses do not belong to you, Ross!

SOLDIER 5:   They belong to your country!

MICKLE: See how long you can stand the heat and smoke!

SOLDIER 3:   Tell your men to surrender!

ROBERT: What men? I'm alone with these horses. Let me command these horses.

               The crackling of flames. Smoke appears. Sounds of agitated horses intensify. Movement within the barn intensifies.

MICKLE: What's he saying?

SOLDIER 3:   He said 'alone.' I told you he's alone.

SOLDIER 6:   When he said 'we' he meant the horses.

               The fire and smoke grows.

ROBERT: What are you doing? Trying to burn us to death? Leave us alone.

               Horses begin to scream.

               Don't do this. All right, all right. You win. I'll let them out.

               ROBERT attempts to unlock the doors.

               The doors are stuck. Let us out!

SOLDIER 6:   Open the damn doors, Lieutenant.

ROBERT: I can't! I can't! I can't!

SOLDIER 5: Just open the damn doors!

ROBERT: I'm trying…but I can't. They're stuck.

SOLDIER 2: Stuck?

MICKLE: Quick, Men! The doors…

ROBERT: Help us!

> *With great difficulty, the soldiers break the doors in with farm tools. The red flare of flames engulfs the barn.*

> *A crescendo of fire and dying horses. ROBERT is on fire. He runs across the field, in flames.*

> *Sudden silence and darkness.*

Scene Eight: Wounds

> *The hospital again. MARIAN is pushing a medical trolley as a young British soldier enters.*

GUARD: Ma'am. Good evening.

MARIAN: Good evening, Corporal. What brings you here tonight?

GUARD: An exceptional case.

MARIAN: What on earth do you mean?

GUARD: A wounded Lieutenant who killed his Superior Officer on the battlefield.

MARIAN: Whatever for?

GUARD: Don't know.

MARIAN: What would lead someone to…?

GUARD: Foolish, really. Probably better not to think too much about these things, ma'am.

MARIAN:　　When?

GUARD:　　A few weeks ago. His condition deteriorated—that's why they sent him here. As soon as he is well enough, he'll be put on trial.

MARIAN:　　I understand.

GUARD:　　I'll be standing watch till then.

MARIAN:　　Very good.

> *Two orderlies carry ROBERT in on a stretcher. ROBERT is almost completely burned from head to toe. Bandages cover his head, hands, and waist. The orderlies move him onto a bed.*

There must be some mistake.

GUARD:　　How do you mean?

MARIAN:　　He's not likely to survive in the condition he is in.

GUARD:　　Even so, when he is well enough, he'll stand trial.

MARIAN:　　It could be a long wait until that day.

GUARD:　　Yes, ma'am. That's why I'm here. To see that he does not escape.

MARIAN:　　Escape? Do you really think he could run away in this condition?

GUARD:　　Ma'am, those are the orders.

MARIAN:　　Where is he going to escape to, might I ask? To a few brief hours of sleep? To death?

GUARD:　　I follow my orders. He can't be trusted.

MARIAN:　　Well, of all the stupid things...covered with burns...the pain must be extraordinary...I don't understand.

GUARD:　　Ma'am. I'll be staying here with the Lieutenant for the next while.

MARIAN: How long have you been in active service, Corporal?

GUARD: Ma'am?

MARIAN: How long?

GUARD: Just over one month.

MARIAN: Have you been in battle yet?

GUARD: No, ma'am. Why?

MARIAN: Nothing.

GUARD: Here are his papers. It's all explained in there.

            The GUARD hands her papers. She reads.

MARIAN: Canadian…Lieutenant Robert Ross…

            MARIAN realizes who he is. Shock. She studies him. The guard takes up his position guarding ROBERT.

            MRS. ROSS appears in a nightgown. A bottle falls from her grasp. She quietly moans.

MRS. ROSS: Help.

            MR. ROSS enters holding a cablegram.

MR. ROSS: …shooting a superior…

MARIAN: …insubordination…

MRS. ROSS: Help.

MR. ROSS: …third degree burns…

MARIAN: …over most of his body…

MR. ROSS: …unable to speak…

MARIAN: …trouble breathing…blistering sores on the left…

MRS. ROSS: Help me.

MR. ROSS: …limited mobility…

MARIAN: …facility to walk questionable…

MR. ROSS: …extraordinary pain…

MRS. ROSS: Help. Darling, where are you?

MR. ROSS: I'm here.

MARIAN: …condition deteriorating….

MR. ROSS: I'm here. Right here.

MRS. ROSS: I'm sorry.

MARIAN: …deteriorating…

MRS. ROSS: Please. I cannot see you.

>   *MR. ROSS moves partway toward her.*

>   I feel like…I've gone…blind.

MR. ROSS: Never mind. Never mind. Here we are.

>   *MR. ROSS holds her. She begins to moan again. ROBERT makes muted whale sounds. The two sounds meld. MR. ROSS and MRS. ROSS fade away.*

MARIAN: Water and Earth and Air and Fire.

GUARD: Pardon?

MARIAN: The very elements that can give life and support life can also destroy life.

GUARD: I don't follow.

MARIAN: No. Corporal, I am short of workers here—would you mind going down the hall and getting me a roll of bandages similar to this one? Lieutenant Ross needs to be changed and I can't go out of the ward. I'm the only one on shift here this evening.

She starts undoing the bandages on ROBERT's arm. The GUARD hesitates.

Please, sir.

The soldier nods. He goes.

Oh, thank you.

She speaks confidentially to ROBERT.

I shouldn't call you by your given name, but I'm going to. Robert, this war is crazy. Not you, or what you did. You must have had your reasons. Good reasons. I'm sure of it.

I want to tell you, after all that I have seen; I am ashamed to be alive. You won't…you can't get better. And they won't ever leave you alone. And they won't forgive you for what you've done. Can you hear me? I can help you. I will help you. I have morphine. More than enough. I've never offered this to anyone before. Not ever. But I want grace for you, Robert.

She pulls out a needle that she has been hiding.

Just give me some sort of indication. I will help you, if you want me to.

After a moment, ROBERT speaks from within the bandages with great effort.

ROBERT: Not…yet.

MARIAN is stunned by his response. After many seconds, she takes his hand.

MARIAN: Not yet.

A poppy field grows.

The End.